TOEFL READING

flash

MILADA BROUKAL

PETERSON'S

THOMSON LEARNING

Australia • Canada • Mexico • Singapore • Spain • United Kingdom • United State

نام‌کتاب: TOEFL READING FLASH

تاریخ و نوبت چاپ: هفتم

ناشر: انتشارات جنگل، جاودانه

تیراژ: ۱۰۰۰۰ نسخه

مجتمع لیتوگرافی، چاپ و صحافی: جنگل

021-66490382-66490465
021-66495275-66486115-9

www.Junglepub.org

CONTENTS

ACKNOWLEDGMENTS

I would like to thank the following professionals for their contribution by reviewing TOEFL® Reading Flash and giving many helpful insights and suggestions:

Paul Abraham, Simmons College
Lida Baker, University of California, Los Angeles
Kelly Franklin, Maryville College
Tom Leverett, Southern Illinois University at Carbondale
Virginia Martin, Bowling Green State University
Nancy Pfingstag, University of North Carolina at Charlotte
Bruce Rogers, Economics Institute

Special thanks to Bruce Rogers for his review and expert proofreading.

I would like to acknowledge sources for some of the passages used in this text. In some cases several sources were used for a passage; in others, the passage was slightly changed in content or style. The following sources were used:

Part One: Types of Reading Comprehension Questions

The source for the sample passage on lie detectors used in the chapters is *Psychology*, by Carole Wade and Carol Tavris (Harper & Row, 1990).

CHAPTER 1

The passage on hermit crabs is based on information from *The Encyclopedia of Aquatic Life*, edited by Dr. Keith Banister and Dr. Andrew Campbell (Facts on File, 1986).

The passage about African-American literature was based on information in *Benet's Reader's Encyclopedia of American Literature*, edited by George Perkins, Barbara Perkins, and Philip Leininger (HarperCollins, 1991).

The source for molecular crystals is based on information from "Building Molecular Crystals," by Paul Fagan and Michael Ward, in *Scientific American*, July 1992.

The passage about education for the colonists and the passage on corporate colonies are based on information in *United States History to 1877*, by Arnold Rice, John Krout, and C. M. Harris (Harper Perennial, 1991).

The source for the passage on cybernetics is based on information from *The New Book of Popular Science*, volume 6 (Grolier; 1987).

The passage on cowboys is based on information from *Cowboy Culture: A Saga of Five Centuries*, by David Dary (Alfred A. Knopf, 1981).

The passage on Mt. St. Helens is based on information from *Mt. St. Helens: The Volcano Explodes*, by Prof. Leonard Palmer and KOIN-TV Newsroom (Northwest Illustrated, 1980).

CHAPTER 2

The passage on the movie *Star Wars* was based on information in *Skywalking: The Life and Films of George Lucas*, by Dale Pollock (Harmony Books, 1983).

The passage on sedimentary rocks is based on information from *The Practical Paleontologist*, by Steve Parker; Raymond Bernor, editor (Simon & Schuster, 1990).

The source for the passage on tennis is from *Tennis: Strokes for Success*, by Doug MacCurdy and Shawn Tully (*Sports Illustrated* Winner's Circle Books, 1988).

The passage on El Nino is based on information from *The Weather Book*, by Jack Williams (Vintage Books, 1992).

The passage on seahorses is based on information from *The Audubon Society Encyclopedia of Animal Life* (Clarkson N. Potter, 1982).

The passage on planes is based on information from *The New Book of Popular Science*, volume 6 (Grolier, 1987).

CHAPTER 3

The passage on cartography is based on information in *The Mapmakers*, by John Noble Wilford (Alfred A. Knopf, 1981).

The passage on California's earthquakes and the passage on Powell's expedition are based on information in *The Shape of the World*, by Simon Berthon and Andrew Robinson (Rand McNally, 1991).

The passage on forests is based on information in *Plant Science*, by Jules Janick, Robert Schery, Frank Woods, and Vernon Ruttan (W. H. Freeman, 1981).

The source for bird songs and calls is based on information in *The Audubon Society Pocket Guides*, edited by Ann H. Whitman (Alfred A. Knopf, 1991).

The passage on Hawaii is based on information in *Hawaii Cookbook & Backyard Luau*, by Elizabeth Toupin (Silvermine Publishers, 1967).

The passage on the history of American painting in the 1820s and 1830s is based on information in *The Story of American Painting*, by Abraham A. Davidson (Harry N. Abrams, 1974).

The passage on the development of railroads is based on information in the *Encyclopedia of American History*, 6th ed., edited by Richard B. Morris (Harper & Row).

The passage on Alaska is based on information in *Wild Alaska*, by Dale Brown and the editors of Time-Life Books (Time-Life Books, 1972).

The passage on the American tradition in literature is based on information in *Benet's Reader's Encyclopedia of American Literature*, edited by George Perkins, Barbara Perkins, and Philip Leininger (HarperCollins, 1991).

CHAPTER 4

The passage on rock and roll is based on information from *Music: An Appreciation*, by Roger Kamien (McGraw-Hill, 1980).

The source for the passage on early immigrants and the passage on the early inhabitants of America are based on information from *United States History to 1877*, by Arnold Rice, John Krout, and C. M. Harris (Harper Perennial, 1991).

The passage on dinosaurs is based on information from *The Complete T Rex*, by John R. Horner and Don Lessem (Simon & Schuster, 1993).

The passage on electronic mail is based on information from *The New Book of Popular Science*, volume 6 (Grolier, 1987).

The passage on brown bears is based on information from *Wild Alaska*, by Dale Brown and the editors of Time-Life Books (Time-Life Books, 1972).

The source for the passage on energy is based on information from *Energy Alternatives*, by Barbara Keeler (Lucent Books, 1990).

CHAPTER 5

The passage on fog is based on information from *The Complete Book of Sailing*, by Robert Bond (Gallery Books, 1990).

The source for the passages on hunger, instinct in human behavior, and mental tests are based on information from *Psychology*, by Carole Wade and Carol Tavris (Harper & Row, 1990).

The passage on the compact disc is based on information from *The New Book of Science*, volume 6 (Grolier, 1987).

The passage on John Muir is based on the article "The John Muir Trail," by Galen Rowell, in *National Geographic*, April 1989.

The passage on African-American culture is based on information in *Benet's Reader's Encyclopedia of American Literature*, edited by George Perkins, Barbara Perkins, and Phillip Leininger (HarperCollins, 1991).

The passage on the industrial robot is based on information in *The New Book of Popular Science*, volume 6 (Grolier, 1987).

The passage on forest fires and the passage on vitamins are based on information in *Plant Science*, by Jules Janick, Robert Schery, Frank Woods, and Vernon Ruttan (W. H. Freeman, 1981).

Part Two: Reading Comprehension Practice Tests

The source for the sample passage is *Psychology*, by Carole Wade and Carol Tavris (Harper & Row, 1990).

PRACTICE TEST 1

The passage on supernovas is based on information in *The Guinness Book of Astronomy*, by Patrick Moore (Guinness).

The passage on Horace Pippin is based on information in *The Story of American Painting*, by Abraham A. Davidson (Harry N. Abrams, 1974).

The passage on the spadefoot toad is based on information in *Arid Lands*, by Jake Page (Time-Life Books, 1984).

The passage on the origin of banking in the United States is based on information in the *Encyclopedia of American History*, 6th ed., edited by Richard B. Morris (Harper & Row).

The passage on the telegraph is based on information in *United States History to 1877*, by Arnold Rice, John Krout, and C. M. Harris (Harper Perennial, 1991).

PRACTICE TEST 2

The passage on Sylvia Earle is based on information in *Current Biography Yearbook 1992*, edited by Judith Graham (H. W. Wilson, 1992).

The passage on farmhouses is based on information in *The American Farmhouse*, by Henry J. Kauffman (Hawthorne Books, 1975).

The passage on geckos is based on information in *The Audubon Society Encyclopedia of Animal Life* (Clarkson N. Potter, 1982).

PRACTICE TEST 3

The passage on dyslexia is from an article by John Rennie in *Scientific American*, July 1992.

The passage on barn owls is based on information from the *Audubon Society Encyclopedia of Animal Life* (Clarkson N. Potter, 1982).

The passage on the laser is based on information in *The New Book of Popular Science*, volume 6 (Grolier, 1987).

The passage on the America's Cup is based on information in *The Complete Book of Sailing*, by Robert Bond (Gallery Books, 1990).

The passage on President Lyndon B. Johnson is based on information in the *Encyclopedia of American History*, 6th ed., edited by Richard B. Morris (Harper & Row).

PRACTICE TEST 4

The passage on ragtime is based on information in *Music: An Appreciation*, by Roger Kamien (McGraw-Hill, 1980).

The passage on the bison is based on information in *The Audubon Society Encyclopedia of Animal Life* (Clarkson N. Potter, 1982).

The passage on the planet Jupiter is based on information in *The Guinness Book of Astronomy*, by Patrick Moore (Guinness).

The passage on computer graphics is based on information in *Computer Graphics*, by Donald Hearn and M. Pauline Baker (Prentice Hall, 1986).

The passage on the Chumash is based on information in *The Chumash*, by Robert O. Gibson (Chelsea House, 1991).

PRACTICE TEST 5

The passage on fiberscopes is based on information in *The New Book of Popular Science*, volume 6 (Grolier, 1987).

The passage on Amy Tan is based on information in *Current Biography Yearbook 1992*, edited by Judith Graham (H. W. Wilson, 1992).

The passage on the continental shelf is based on information in *The Northeast Coast*, by Maitland A. Edey (Time-Life Books, 1972).

The passage on the Constitution is based on information in *United States History to 1877*, by Arnold Rice, John Krout, and C. M. Harris (Harper Perennial, 1991).

The passage on tortoises is based on information in *The Audubon Society Encyclopedia of Animal Life* (Clarkson N. Potter, 1982).

TO THE TEACHER

The *TOEFL® Reading Flash* is a preparation book for the Reading Comprehension section of the TOEFL®. It can be both used in a classroom and assigned for self-study to a student who needs more work on reading. It can also be used in the classroom with assignments being given for homework.

The first section of the book concentrates on the types of reading questions on the TOEFL®. Each chapter in this section is devoted to a certain type of question. The first chapters cover all the types of questions found on the TOEFL® test. These have been sequenced in order of difficulty, beginning with the easiest types of questions, "Reading for Details," and ending with the most difficult, "Reading for Inference." Although the reading questions reflect skills needed for the test, they are also basic reading skills: reading for main ideas, reading for details, making inferences, vocabulary in context, and so on. There are numerous readings in the exercises that follow each type of question to provide the student with plenty of practice in reading on a variety of topics typical of those found on the actual exam. The reading passages have been selected to reflect the ones on the actual exam in terms of length, style, vocabulary, and content.

The second section of the book contains five Reading Comprehension practice tests. These may be used as assessment tests through a period of study. An answer key is provided, with annotations give for one complete test.

Structure of Each Chapter

A. Introduction

- **Prereading Questions** Prereading questions that will involve the students in thinking about and anticipating the topic precede the reading passage.

- **Reading Passage** A reading passage that is not like the TOEFL® introduces the chapter to provide a topic of discussion or interest.

- **Comprehension Questions** General comprehension questions, including the question type to be practiced in the chapter, are introduced. The questions in this part are not like those of the TOEFL®. They can be answered orally or in writing or used in group work.

  The question types following each passage are accumulative as one advances through the chapters. In other words, the first chapter has detail questions following the passage; the second chapter has reference and vocabulary as well as detail questions following the passage.

- **Discussion** Discussion questions on the reading topic provide classroom interaction.

B. The Question Type

- **Definition** The question type is explained, and examples of the questions are give.

- **Sample Passage** One sample reading passage is used through all the chapters. An example question and an annotated answer are given.

- **Strategies** Strategies or helpful tips are provided for the student before he or she starts on the exercises.

C. Exercises

- **Passages with questions** Passages on a variety of topics similar to those found on the TOEFL® followed by questions of the type covered in the chapter make up the exercises.

TO THE STUDENT

You can use this book alone or with a teacher to prepare for the Reading Comprehension Section of the TOEFL®. Each chapter covers a type of reading question that you will find on the TOEFL®. The first part of each chapter introduces the question through a reading passage. This passage is easier than the passages on the TOEFL®. Its purpose is to introduce you to the type of question you will study in the chapter. Then, the second part of each chapter tells you in detail about the type of question, giving examples and suggesting strategies. It is important that you read this part carefully before doing the exercises that follow. Finally, the exercises in the third part will give you plenty of practice in reading on a variety of topics and in answering questions similar to those found on the TOEFL® test.

To practice for the Reading Comprehension section of the exam, it is important to take practice tests. There are five practice Reading Comprehension tests in this book. Each time you take a test, pretend it is the actual exam. Time yourself. Do not spend more than 1 minute (60 seconds) on a question. After you have finished a test, check the answers at the back of the book. Learn from your mistakes so that the next time you take the test you will not make the same mistake again.

INTRODUCTION

THE READING COMPREHENSION SECTION OF THE TOEFL®

This section contains five or six reading passages, each followed by 4 to 8 questions for a total of 30 questions. The passages vary in length from about 800 words to about 1,500. The topics of the passages cover subjects that might be studied in an American university, such as American history, geography, astronomy, geology, literature, art, economics, psychology, sociology, zoology, and biographies of historical figures or famous scientists or artists.

General Strategies

To improve your reading speed and comprehension, remember these general points:

- **Read as widely as possible.** Read on as many topics as you can. The more you read the better a reader you will be. You will in this way be exposed to a greater vocabulary.
- **Read carefully and critically.** Ask yourself reading comprehension questions as you are reading.

What is the main idea?

What are the details?

What can be inferred?

What conclusions can be drawn?

What can this word mean?

What is the purpose of the author?

The following are some strategies to help you with the Reading Comprehension questions.

Strategies for Answering Reading Comprehension Questions

- **Read the question first.** Read the question, not the answer choices. When you know the kinds of questions you must answer, it will be easier to find the answers.
- **Skim or read the passage quickly.** Do not read word for word or in detail. Read quickly to find the main idea and general organization.
- **Go back to the passage to answer questions.** If you know the answer, you do not need to go back to the passage.
- **Leave the difficult questions until last.**
- **Take a guess when you do not know the answer.** If you do not know the answer, take a guess. When you are taking a guess, first use a process of elimination. How can you eliminate the wrong answer on a multiple-choice item?

All multiple-choice questions on the TOEFL® follow the same principle. There is one stem and four answer choices. One choice is correct, and the three incorrect choices are distracters. In other words, they distract you, or take your attention away from the correct answer.

Stem . . .

    (A) Incorrect
    (B) Correct
    (C) Incorrect
    (D) Incorrect

One of the distracters is almost correct, and the other two are more clearly incorrect. You can eliminate these two clearly incorrect choices.

Stem . . .

    (A) Almost correct
    (B) Correct
    (C) Incorrect
    (D) Incorrect

If you cannot decide between the almost correct answer and the correct answer, take a guess. You may have an intuitive or unexplained feeling that one answer is correct. Use your intuition when you cannot decide.

If you do not know the answer and do not have a feeling about the correct answer, use a guess letter (A, B, C, or D). Use the same letter to answer every item you do not know. Using the same letter will give you a better chance to get a correct answer.

- **Answer all questions.** Never leave any items unanswered. If you have no time left, use your guess letter.

PART ONE

Types of Reading Comprehension Questions

CHAPTER 1 READING FOR DETAILS

Introducing Details
PREREADING QUESTIONS

Answer the following questions.

1. What do you know about hairstyles in ancient times?
2. What kinds of things to do you think people did to their hair in ancient times?
3. Do you think that hairstyles and colors were important for both men and women?

Line   People have been concerned with their hair since ancient times. In 1500 B.C., the Assyrians, inhabiting the area know today as Northern Iraq, were the world's first true hairstylists. Their skills at cutting, curling, layering and dyeing hair were known throughout the Middle East. In fact,
5   they were obsessed with their hair, which was oiled, perfumed, and tinted. A fashionable courtier wore his hair cut in neat geometric layers. Kings, soldiers, and noblewomen had their hair curled with a fire-heated iron bar, probably the world's first curling iron. So important was hair styling in Assyria that law dictated certain types of hairstyles according to
10   a person's position and employment. Facial hair was also important. Men grew beards down to their chests and had them clipped in layers. High-ranking women in both Egypt and Assryia wore fake beards during official court business to show their equal authority with men.
     Like the Assyrians, the early Greeks liked long, scented, curly hair.
15   Fair hair was favored over dark, so those who were not "natural blonds" lightened or reddened their hair with soaps and bleaches. The Romans, on the other hand, favored dark hair for men for high social or political rank. Early Saxon men were neither blonds nor brunets but dyed their hair and beards blue, red, green, and orange.
20   Over the centuries, societies have combed, curled, waved, powdered, dyed, cut, coiffed, and sculpted their hair, or someone else's during times of wig crazes. Churches and lawmakers have sometimes tried to put a stop to the human obsession with hair, but with little success. It seems hairstyling is here to stay, and the future will likely prove no exception.

Exercise 1

> **Answer the following questions.**

SKIMMING
Read the passage quickly once again.

1. What is the passage about?

SCANNING
Look over the article again to find the answers to questions 2-13.

Complete the following sentences with details from the passage.

2. The hairstyling skills of the Assyrians were known all over _____ .

3. An Assyrian courtier had his hair _____ .

4. The Assyrians had laws for certain types of hairstyles according to people's _____ and _____ .

5. During official court business women in Egypt wore _____ .

6. _____ preferred fair hair.

7. _____ preferred dark hair for men of high rank.

Locate the following details in the passage. Give the line numbers.

8. In which lines does the author explain how people curled their hair?

9. In which lines does the author first mention changing the color of hair?

10. At what point in the passage does the author discuss the wearing of wigs?

Underline the detail that is NOT mentioned in the passage in each of the sentences below.

11. The kings, soldiers, and women of Assyria curled their hair.

12. The Assyrians and the Greeks liked long, perfumed, blond, curly hair.

13. Beards were important for the Assyrians, Egyptians, and Greeks.

Detail Questions

Detail questions ask you about specific information in the passage. Detail questions usually begin with the words

ACCORDING TO THE PASSAGE . . .

To answer detail questions, focus on the key word or words used in the question. Then you must scan the passage. When you scan a passage, you move your eyes quickly over the passage until you find the key words that you are looking for: a name, a date, a number. It is not necessary to read the whole passage again—just locate the key words. Once you find the key words, you can read the sentences that follow or come before to make sure you have found the right information.

The correct answer to a detail question will not usually use the exact words as found in the passage but synonyms or a restatement of what is stated in the passage. For example, if the passage states that "Eugene O'Neill was a well-known dramatist," the answer to a question about the kind of work he was known for might state that "his plays won him fame."

Detail questions usually appear in the order of the information presented in the passage. This means that the answer to the first detail question will come near the beginning of the passage and the information for the second question will come after that.

Sample Reading Passage

Line   Although "lie detectors" are being used by governments, police
departments, and businesses that all want guaranteed ways of detecting
the truth, the results are not always accurate. Lie detectors are properly
called emotion detectors, for their aim is to measure bodily changes that
5   contradict what a person says. The polygraph machine records changes in
heart rate, breathing, blood pressure, and the electrical activity of the skin
(galvanic skin response, or GSR). In the first part of the polygraph test, you
are electronically connected to the machine and asked a few neutral
questions ("What is your name?" "Where do you live?"). Your physical
10   reactions serve as the standard (baseline) for evaluating what comes next.
Then you are asked a few critical questions among the neutral ones
("When did you rob the bank?"). The assumption is that if you are guilty,
your body will reveal the truth, even if you try to deny it. Your heart rate,
respiration, and GSR will change abruptly as you respond to the
15   incriminating questions.

That is the theory; but psychologists have found that lie detectors are
simply not reliable. Since most physical changes are the same across all
emotions, machines cannot tell whether you are feeling guilty, angry,
nervous, thrilled, or revved up from an exciting day. Innocent people may
20   be tense and nervous about the whole procedure. They may react
physiologically to a certain word ("bank") not because they robbed it, but

because they recently bounced a check. In either case the machine will record a "lie." The reverse mistake is also common. Some practiced liars can lie without flinching, and others learn to beat the machine by tensing
25   muscles or thinking about an exciting experience during neutral questions.

QUESTION

1. According to the passage, polygraph tests

   (A) record a person's physical reactions
   (B) measure a person's thoughts
   (C) always reveal the truth about a person
   (D) make guilty people angry

ANSWER

Answer (A) is correct because it is a rewording of "bodily changes." Answer (B) is incorrect because the polygraph measures physical changes; thoughts are not physical changes. Answer (C) is also incorrect since the passage states that lie detectors are "simply not reliable." Answer (D) is incorrect since the polygraph does not make guilty people nervous; it makes innocent people nervous.

QUESTION

1. According to the passage, what kind of questions are asked on the first part of the polygraph test?

   (A) Critical
   (B) Unimportant
   (C) Incriminating
   (D) Emotional

ANSWER

Answer (A) is not correct because critical questions are asked on the second part of the test. Answer (C) is also not correct since incriminating questions are not asked on the first part of the test. Answer (D) is also incorrect since "What is your name?" and "Where do you live?" are not emotional questions. The best answer is (B), which is another word for "neutral."

DETAIL QUESTIONS ABOUT WHAT IS NOT IN THE PASSAGE

This type of detail question asks about what is not in the passage or what is not true according to the passage. These questions have the word NOT or EXCEPT in capital letters. The following are examples of such questions:

Which of the following is NOT mentioned in the passage?
According to the passage, all of the following are true EXCEPT. . . .

In this type of question, three of the answers are true and one of the answers is not mentioned in the passage or is not true. Scan the passage to find the answers that are true or stated in the passage. The answer that is not mentioned in the passage or is not true is the correct one.

Read the sample reading passage again.

QUESTION

1. Which of the following is NOT mentioned as something that is measured by a polygraph machine?

   (A) Blood pressure
   (B) Heart rate
   (C) Breathing
   (D) Eye movement

Remember, three of the answers are mentioned and one is not mentioned.

ANSWER

(A) is mentioned because the passage states that the polygraph records changes in blood pressure. Because (A) is mentioned, it is not the correct answer. (B) is also mentioned because the passage states that the polygraph machine records changes in heart rate. Since (B) is mentioned, it is not correct. Answer (C) is also mentioned, because the passage states that the polygraph machine records breathing. Since (C) is mentioned it is not correct. The best answer to the question is therefore (D) because it is not mentioned.

Strategies for Answering Detail Questions

- The answers to detail questions will follow the order of information presented in the passage.
- The correct answers to detail questions are often a restatement of what is stated in the passage.
- If the question has the word NOT or EXCEPT, choose the answer that is not true or not mentioned in the passage. Answers that are true or mentioned in the passage are not correct.

Exercises on Details

Exercise 2

> **Read the passages and answer the detail questions that follow each one.**

QUESTIONS 1–6

Hermit crabs occupy the empty shells of dead sea snails for protection while still retaining their mobility. They are capable of discriminating among a selection of shells of various sizes and species, and they choose the one that fits the body most closely. Hermit crabs change shells as they grow, although in some marine environments a large enough variety of shells may not be available and the hermit crab may be forced to occupy a smaller-than-ideal "house." When a shell becomes too small for the hermit crab to occupy, it will sometimes become aggressive and fight other hermit crabs to gain a larger shell.

Hermit crabs may encounter empty shells in the course of their daily activity, but the vacant shell is usually spotted by sight. The hermit crab's visual response increases with the size of an object and its contrast against the background. The hermit crab then seizes the shell with its walking legs and climbs on it, monitoring its size. If the size is right, the crab investigates its shape and texture by rolling it over between its walking legs and running its claws over the surface. Once the shell's opening has been located, the crab uses its claws to remove any foreign material before preparing to enter. The crab rises above the opening, flexes its abdomen, and enters the shell backward. The shell interior is monitored by the abdomen as the crab repeatedly enters and withdraws. When completely satisfied with its new mobile home, the hermit crab will emerge one last time, turn the shell over and make a final entrance.

1. According to the passage, hermit crabs occupy vacant shells for

   (A) mobility
   (B) flexibility
   (C) protection
   (D) discrimination

2. According to the passage, a hermit crab changes shells when it

   (A) outgrows the one it has
   (B) hunts for food
   (C) becomes aggressive
   (D) locates any vacant shell

3. According to the passage, the way in which hermit crabs locate empty shells is through which of the following senses?

   (A) Hearing
   (B) Touch
   (C) Taste
   (D) Sight

4. A crab investigates a vacant shell for all of the following EXCEPT

   (A) size
   (B) type
   (C) shape
   (D) texture

5. According to the passage. a hermit crab enters a new shell

   (A) head first
   (B) claws first
   (C) backward
   (D) with its walking legs

6. According to the passage, a hermit crab settles into its new "mobile home"

   (A) after entering and leaving several times
   (B) without inspecting the interior first
   (C) immediately after locating the shell opening
   (D) after fighting other hermit crabs for a larger shell

QUESTIONS 7–13

The first black literature in America was not written but was preserved in an oral tradition, in a rich body of folklore, songs and stories, many from African origins. There are humorous tales, Biblical stories, animal stories, and stories of natural phenomena, of good and bad people, and of the wise and foolish. Many reflect how African Americans viewed themselves and their lives. The lyrics of blues, spirituals, and work songs speak of suffering and hope, joy and pain, loved ones, and religious faith, and are an integral part of the early literature of black people in America.

The earliest existing written black literature was Lucy Terry's poem "Bars Fight," written in 1746. Other eighteenth-century black poets include Jupiter Hammon and George Moses Horton. The first African American to publish a book in American was Phillis Wheatley. Black poetry also flourished in the nineteenth-century, during which the writings of almost forty poets were printed, the most notable of whom was Paul Laurence Dunbar, the first black American to achieve national acclaim for his work. Dunbar published eight volumes of poetry and eight novels and collections of stories.

More than three dozen novels were written by blacks between 1853 and 1899, but autobiography dominated African-American literature in the nineteenth-century, as it had in the eighteenth. In the twentieth century, however, fiction has presided, with Charles W. Chestnutt, America's first black man of letters, successfully bridging the two centuries. He began publishing short fiction in the mid-1880s, wrote two books that appeared in 1899, and had three books published between 1900 and 1905. He was a pioneer of the "new literature" of the early 1900s, which aimed to persuade readers of the worth and equality of African Americans.

7. Which of the following is NOT mentioned in the passage as part of the oral tradition of African Americans?

   (A) Humorous tales
   (B) Tales of adventure
   (C) Biblical stories
   (D) Animal stories

8. According to the passage, the lyrics of blues and spirituals are often concerned with

   (A) the pain and joy in life
   (B) loved ones and animals
   (C) religion and nature
   (D) wise and foolish people

9. According to the passage, an important part of early African-American literature was

   (A) novels
   (B) short fiction stories
   (C) biographies
   (D) songs

10. According to the passage, when did the first written African-American literature appear?

   (A) In the 1600s
   (B) In the 1700s
   (C) In the 1800s
   (D) In the 1900s

11. According to the passage, who was the first African American to receive national recognition for his writing?

   (A) Paul Dunbar
   (B) George Horton
   (C) Lucy Terry
   (D) Phillis Wheatley

12. According to the passage, what form dominated African-American literature in the nineteenth century?

(A) Poetry
(B) Novels
(C) Autobiography
(D) Fiction

13. According to the passage, Charles W. Chestnutt was one the first writers to

(A) write about the suffering of African Americans
(B) publish short fiction in the early 1990s
(C) write persuasively about the worth of African Americans
(D) dominate the African-American literary tradition

QUESTIONS 14–20

A snowflake originates from countless water molecules that initially come together in small groups as a result of a weak attractive force between oxygen and hydrogen atoms. The same forces subsequently organize the groups into a frozen molecular crystal, a perfectly organized lattice of molecules. Finally, several molecular crystals join to form a snowflake. Scientists have realized for some time that the forces that assemble molecules into natural crystals can be utilized to produce a variety of important materials. They have determined the structure of more than 90,000 different molecular crystals, the most common examples of which are aspirin and mothballs.

In recent years, researchers have studied how molecules organize themselves to form crystals in the hope of better understanding what types of molecules and what conditions will produce molecular crystals with unusual and useful properties. Scientists are aware that the material properties of a crystal depend in large part on the organization of the molecules in the crystal, yet they know little about the factors controlling the assembly of such crystals.

Synthesizing a molecular crystal is similar to designing a building. Before construction can begin, the architect must specify the shapes and sizes of the girders and the number and placement of the rivets. Similarly, to produce new molecular crystals, chemists must choose molecules of the appropriate sizes and shapes and select the molecular forces that will hold the crystals together. A chemist can normally find many molecules of various shapes and sizes, but the challenge is to find ones that assemble in a predictable manner.

14. According to the passage, a snowflake is formed by

(A) the attractive force between oxygen and hydrogen
(B) molecular crystals with new and useful properties
(C) the synthesizing of molecular crystals
(D) the joining of several molecular crystals

15. According to the passage, water molecules join together as a result of

    (A) an attraction between oxygen and hydrogen atoms
    (B) the organization of the molecules in a crystal
    (C) a strong force that assembles crystal atoms
    (D) the unusual and useful properties of molecular crystals

16. By making use of forces that assemble molecules into natural crystals, scientists can

    (A) find molecules of various shapes and sizes
    (B) determine the structure of different molecular crystals
    (C) organize molecules into a perfect lattice
    (D) create new and useful materials

17. According to the passage, what reason do researchers have for studying how molecules organize themselves to form crystals?

    (A) To assemble molecules into natural crystals
    (B) To learn how to synthesize molecular crystals
    (C) To make aspirin and mothballs
    (D) To change the material properties of a crystal

18. According to the passage, what do scientists still need to learn about the organization of molecules?

    (A) What determines the material property of a crystal
    (B) The molecular forces that hold molecules together
    (C) The conditions that produce molecular crystals
    (D) The factors controlling the way crystals are assembled

19. To produce new molecular crystals, chemists must choose all of the following EXCEPT

    (A) molecules of the right size
    (B) molecules of the appropriate shape
    (C) the right molecular organization
    (D) the proper molecular forces

20. According to the passage, the task of synthesizing a molecular crystal can be compared to

    (A) designing a building
    (B) building a house
    (C) making materials
    (D) constructing a lattice

QUESTIONS 21–28

   Education was of primary importance to the English colonists and was conducted at home as well as in established schools. Regardless of geographic location or finances, most Americans learned to read and compute numbers. For many, the Bible and other religious tracts were their only books; however, the excellent language contained in such works usually made them good primers. Many families owned one or more of Shakespeare's works, a copy of John Bunyan's classic *A Pilgrim's Progress*, and sometimes collections of English literary essays, poems, or historical speeches.

   In 1647 the Massachusetts School Law required every town of at least 50 households to maintain a grammar school. The law was the first to mandate public education in America. In the middle colonies at the time, schools were often dependent on religious societies, such as the Quakers and other private organizations. In the South, families employed private tutors or relied on the clergy to conduct education. At the outset, most elementary schools were for boys, but schools for girls were established in the eighteenth century in most cities and large towns. In spite of the informal atmosphere of most American schools, the literacy rate in the colonies of mid-eighteenth-century America was equal to or higher than in most European countries.

   Before the American Revolution, nine colleges had been founded, including Harvard, William and Mary, Yale, the College of New Jersey (now Princeton), Brown, Rutgers, Dartmouth, and Kings College (later Columbia University). By 1720 the natural sciences and modern languages were being taught, as well as courses in practical subjects such as mechanics and agriculture. At the end of the eighteenth century, medical schools were established at the College of Philadelphia and at King's College.

21. Which of the following words best describes the English colonists' attitude toward education?

    (A) Indifferent
    (B) Distrustful
    (C) Enthusiastic
    (D) Casual

22. According to the passage, most Americans learned how to

    (A) write
    (B) read
    (C) farm
    (D) speak a foreign language

23. According to the passage, all of the following sometimes substituted for school books EXCEPT

    (A) historical speeches
    (B) works of Shakespeare
    (C) literary essays
    (D) biographies

24. According to the passage, the Massachusetts School Law applied to every town with how many households?

(A) Less than fifty
(B) Exactly fifty
(C) Fifty or more
(D) Fifteen

25. According to the passage, the middle colonies often depended upon which group to provide education?

(A) Private organizations
(B) Colleges
(C) Established primary schools
(D) Businesses

26. According to the passage, who often conducted education in the South?

(A) Public school teachers
(B) Doctors
(C) Clergy
(D) Politicians

27. How well educated were Americans in comparison to most European countries?

(A) Much worse
(B) The same or better
(C) Far better
(D) Less or equal

28. According to the passage, all the following subjects are mentioned as being taught in colleges in the 1700s EXCEPT

(A) languages
(B) science
(C) medicine
(D) economics

QUESTIONS 29-36

The study of control processes in electronic, mechanical, and biological systems is known as cybernetics. The word was coined in 1948 by the American mathematician Norbert Wiener from the Greek word meaning pilot or steersman. Cybernetics is concerned with the analysis of the flow of information in both living organisms and machines, but it is particularly concerned with systems that are capable of regulating their own operations without human control.

Automatic regulation is accomplished by using information about the state of the end product that is fed back to the regulating device, causing it to modify or correct production procedures if necessary. The concept of feedback is at the very heart of cybernetics and is what makes a system automatic and self-regulating. A simple example of a self-regulating machine is a thermostat, which reacts to continual feedback about the outside temperature and responds accordingly to achieve the temperature that has been programmed into it.

The applications of cybernetics are wide reaching, appearing in science, engineering, technology, sociology, economics, education, and medicine. Computers can keep a patient alive during a surgical operation, making instantaneous modifications based on a constant flow of information. In education, teaching machines use cybernetic principles to instruct students on an individual basis. In the home, automation is present in such everyday products as refrigerators, coffeemakers, and dishwashers. In industry, automation is increasing its applications, although it is currently applied primarily to the large-scale production of single units. In industries in which a break in the flow of production can ruin the product, automatic controls are invaluable. Chemical and petroleum plants are now almost completely automatic, as are industries involved in the production of chemicals and atomic energy. Automation has become the answer when human safety is the number one priority.

29. Cybernetics is the study of control processes in all of the systems EXCEPT

   (A) ecological
   (B) biological
   (C) mechanical
   (D) electronic

30. According to the passage, the word "cybernetics" was coined from the Greek word meaning

   (A) information
   (B) automatic
   (C) pilot
   (D) regulator

31. According to the passage, cybernetics is primarily concerned with systems that

   (A) are controlled by humans
   (B) analyze flaws of information
   (C) are self-regulating
   (D) have wide-reaching applications

32. According to the passage, how is automatic regulation accomplished?

   (A) By modifying and correcting production procedures
   (B) By feeding information to the regulatory device
   (C) By analyzing the flow of information to the organism
   (D) By making modifications in cybernetic principles

33. According to the passage, what makes a system automatic and self-regulating?

    (A) Information
    (B) Production procedures
    (C) Human control
    (D) Feedback

34. Which of the following is NOT mentioned as an area in which cybernetics has applications?

    (A) Technology
    (B) Engineering
    (C) Philosophy
    (D) Education

35. According to the passage, automation in industry is primarily used in producing

    (A) large quantities of a single unit
    (B) everyday household products
    (C) small amounts of many different products
    (D) high-tech surgical instruments

36. According to the passage, automation is extremely important when the top priority is

    (A) efficiency
    (B) speed
    (C) convenience
    (D) safety

QUESTIONS 37–44

Cattle ranchers throughout the American West owe much of their traditional culture to the Spaniards, who first introduced cattle to the New World and first developed cattle ranching in the Western Hemisphere. The vaquero, or Mexican cowboy, was born of the necessity to look after the cattle that grazed open ranges. He was not a romantic figure but a poor laborer on horseback, who wore what clothes he had on his back and eventually found certain types of dress more appropriate than others, a blend of Spanish dress and that worn by the natives.

Working in the hot sun brought the adoption of Spanish sombreros and bandannas. Because it was waterproof and wind resistant, leather was eventually the chosen material for jackets and leggings, or botas, the predecessor to chaps. A large pair of iron spurs were the badge of the vaquero, and a *lazo* (lasso)—a rope with slipknot—was the vaquero's primary working tool, especially on the trail drives that became commonplace by the sixteenth century. Saddle makers added a large saddle horn to the Spanish saddle to accommodate the lasso during the roping technique, in which the vaquero tossed the rope around the cow and then quickly tied and wrapped the end of the rope around the horn. Later, American cowboys north of the Rio Grande learned this technique.

As the size of cattle herds grew and rustlers became a problem, the Spanish cattlemen asked the authorities to put a stop to them. The Spanish crown responded with the establishment of the Mesta to enact ordinances to benefit and increase the herds and to remedy and punish crimes. The Mesta served the special interests of cattle raisers and preceded the American West's cattlemen's associations. Moreover the Mesta's ordinances were similar to modern American laws relating to ranching, and today's laws, in fact, are essentially variations and adaptations of the regulations first established in the New World more than four centuries ago.

37. According to the passage, which of the following best describes the vaquero?

   (A) A romantic figure
   (B) A wealthy cattle rancher
   (C) A poor working man
   (D) A Spanish explorer

38. According to the passage, who introduced cattle to the Western Hemisphere?

   (A) The American cowboys
   (B) The Spaniards
   (C) The Mexicans
   (D) The native Americans

39. According to the passage, what kind of clothing was worn by the Mexican cowboy?

   (A) A combination of formal and informal dress
   (B) A variation on the style worn by American cattlemen
   (C) The same type of garments the cowboys wore in their villages
   (D) A blend of native and Spanish dress

40. According to the passage, what element of nature inspired the vaqueros to wear hats and bandannas?

   (A) Sun
   (B) Wind
   (C) Rain
   (D) Cold

41. According to the passage, leather was chosen as the material for a cowboy's jacket and leggings because

    (A) it was warm
    (B) it was waterproof
    (C) it made good padding for horseback riding
    (D) it was good protection from the sun

42. According to the passage, which of the following is NOT mentioned as being among a vaquero's possessions during trail drives?

    (A) A pair of spurs
    (B) A lass.
    (C) A pair of botas
    (D) A pair of leather gloves

43. According to the passage, why did saddle makers eventually put a horn on the Spanish saddle?

    (A) To make a place on which to tie the lasso
    (B) So the cowboy would have something to hold onto
    (C) To add something to hang things on
    (D) To make it easier to get on and off the horse

44. According to the passage, the ordinances enacted by the Mesta

    (A) were meant to protect the working cowboy
    (B) protected the rights of the natives
    (C) were to serve the interests of the cattle ranchers
    (D) were eliminated when American ranching laws were passed

QUESTIONS 45–49

May 18, 1980, dawned clear and cool in the Cascades, but it would pass into history as a momentous day when the cataclysmic eruption of Mt. St. Helens turned a vast area of the pristine Washington countryside into a cauldron of devastation. Mt. St. Helens was one of the most beautiful mountains in the Northwest, having been called the Fujiyama of America, but it was also, and still remains, the most active volcano in the Cascade Range.

A century of volcanic inactivity has made Washingtonians complacent. However, beneath the tranquil sylvan paradise, molten magma was slowly rising to the surface of the earth, eventually forming a mushroom-shaped lava dome that exploded with the force of 10 million tons of TNT at 8:30 a.m., throwing nature into upheaval. A hot plume of ash and debris rose 65,000 feet into the sky, turning day into night. Billowing, hot molten rock avalanches swept down the flanks of the mountain, mowing down everything in their paths. Spirit Lake boiled, and rivers turned black. On the slopes great swaths of trees were blown away from the mountain and tossed in heaps. Fires burned everywhere. In the aftermath, what had been pristine beauty only hours before lay in total devastation. The crest of the mountain had been completely blown away and a thick carpet of ash covered the landscape. Trees were strewn about like toothpicks. There were no signs of life.

Most people believed that decades, even centuries, would pass before the land would recover. However, nature proved to be far more resilient than expected. The return of life, both plant and animal, was remarkable, and today undergrowth carpets the ground and wildlife is abundant. A forest of young trees graces the slopes and valleys below the volcano, and a delicate and serene beauty has returned once more to this vast wilderness area.

45. According to the passage, Mt. St. Helens was called the Fujiyama of America because of its

    (A) height
    (B) beauty
    (C) volcanic activity
    (D) cataclysmic eruption

46. According to the passage, what was the mood of Washingtonians before the eruption occurred?

    (A) They had been expecting the eruption for some time.
    (B) They didn't know that Mt. St. Helens was an active volcano.
    (C) They knew that whatever happened, nature would recover.
    (D) They were not concerned about the eruption at all.

47. According to the passage, how long had Mt. St. Helens been inactive?

    (A) Ten years
    (B) Fifty years
    (C) One hundred years
    (D) Two hundred years

48. When Mt. St. Helens exploded, which of the following did NOT occur?

    (A) Molten rock avalanches flowed down mountainsides.
    (B) A plume of ash and debris rose to the sky.
    (C) The earth cracked and formed a new valley.
    (D) Fires burned in the forests.

49. According to the passage, what does the Mt. St. Helens area look like today?

    (A) Nature has made a surprising recovery.
    (B) The land is as devastated as it was the day of the eruption.
    (C) Nature has not proven to be very resilient.
    (D) There is undergrowth but no trees.

LOCATING DETAILS

In some detail questions you are asked where in the passage a particular piece of information is located. The answers to this type of question are line numbers.
  The following are examples of questions for locating details:

At what point in the passage does the author discuss . . . ?

Where in the passage does the author first mention . . . ?

In which lines does the author explain . . . ?

To answer such questions, scan the passage looking for the key words using the same technique as for detail questions.
  Read the sample reading passage again (p. 4).

QUESTION

1. Where in the passage does the author first mention how the test is given?

    (A) Lines 3-4
    (B) Lines 4-5
    (C) Lines 5-7
    (D) Lines 7-9

ANSWER

Answer (A) is incorrect because lines 3-4 only mention another name for lie detectors. Answer (B) is also incorrect because in lines 4-5 only the purpose or aim of lie detectors is mentioned. Answer (C) also is incorrect because lines 5-7 state only what the machine records, not how it works. The best answer to the question is (D), lines 7-9, which state that "you are electronically connected to the machine and asked a few neutral questions" and are therefore the first mention of how a polygraph works.

QUESTION

1. In which lines does the author explain how some people learn to trick the polygraph?

    (A) Lines 17-19
    (B) Lines 19-20
    (C) Lines 20-22
    (D) Lines 23-26

ANSWER

Answer (A) is incorrect because lines 17-19 state how the machine can be unreliable. Answer (B) is also incorrect since lines 19-20 mention only innocent people and not how they can trick the machine. Answer (C) is also incorrect because lines 20-22 only mention how innocent people may react to the machine. The best answer is (D), lines 23-26, which state how "some practiced liars" learn to "beat the machine" and in this way trick the polygraph.

EXERCISE 3

Read the following passages and answer the questions on locating details that follow.

QUESTIONS 1–7

Line   Mineral King, located at the southern edge of Sequoia National Park in California, is a glacially carved valley situated along the headwaters of the east fork of the Kaweah River, at an altitude of 7,800 feet. The steep, sparsely forested slopes of rusty mineral-rich rock surrounding the valley

5   gave Mineral King its name and twice nearly destroyed its isolated tranquility.

The first instance occurred in 1872 after a hunter named Harry O'Farrell spied silver and mineral deposits and hastily staked his claim. Within a year, ninety-three prospectors had filed claims and the Mineral

10   King Mining District was formed. During the rest of the decade the valley resembled a boomtown, complete with assay office, bakeshop, barbershop, post office, general store, and cabins, and the population rose to 300. A toll road, tramway, and smelter were built, but only one silver ingot was even produced. Moreover, year after year winter avalanches hit the

15   mines, destroying cabins, shops, the stamp mill, and the tramway. Discouraged, the miners finally admitted defeat in 1881.

For years the area slumbered serenely in its obscurity, until 1969, when the Forest Service granted a permit to Disney Enterprises, which had plans for a momumental project replete with an Alpine village of hotels,

20   theaters and restaurants, a ski area designed to serve 10,000 people a day, and proposals for a cog railway, an aerial tramway, and a monorail. Environmentalists and wilderness enthusiasts were horrified, and ten years of court battles ensued. It was Nature, however, who had the final say, delivering avalanche after avalanche over cabins, snow deflection barriers,

25   and even a platform-mounted gun that was meant to trigger slides when they were still small. In 1978 Disney abandoned its grand plan and Mineral King was added to Sequoia National Park, its raw beauty and isolated tranquility protected forever.

1. At what point in the passage does the author specifically discuss the reasons why the miners left Mineral King?

    (A) Lines 10–12
    (B) Lines 14–16
    (C) Line 17
    (D) Lines 26–28

2. Where in the passage does the author first mention Disney's plans for Mineral King?

   (A) Line 17
   (B) Lines 18-21
   (C) Lines 22-23
   (D) Lines 26-28

3. In which lines does the author first describe Mineral King?

   (A) Lines 1-3
   (B) Lines 3-6
   (C) Lines 7-8
   (D) Lines 9-10

4. Where in the passage does the author mention the deciding factor in the final outcome of the Disney plans?

   (A) Lines 17-19
   (B) Lines 22-23
   (C) Lines 23-26
   (D) Lines 26-28

5. At what point in the passage does the author describe the look of Mineral King Valley during its occupation by the miners?

   (A) Lines 3-6
   (B) Lines 9-10
   (C) Lines 10-12
   (D) Lines 15-16

6. Where in the passage does the author describe the reaction of environmentalists to the Disney proposal?

   (A) Lines 15-16
   (B) Lines 22-23
   (C) Lines 23-26
   (D) Lines 26-28

7. In which lines does the author explain how Mineral King got its name?

   (A) Lines 1-3
   (B) Lines 3-6
   (C) Lines 7-8
   (D) Lines 7-10

QUESTIONS 8–13
Line   Between 1607 and 1732 permanent English settlements were established
       along the eastern coast of North America. The new colonies provided
       havens for immigrants avoiding persecution and punishment, business
       failures, or poor prospects for trade and work in the mother country. The
5   English government authorized the use of two kinds of agencies to
       promote the establishment of settlements overseas: the chartered trading
       company and the proprietorship.
              The commercial joint-stock companies operating under royal
       charters were composed of adventuresome stockholders, who shared the
10   profits and losses of their colonial venture. Two of the colonies established
       by English chartered trading companies were Jamestown, Virginia, and the
       Puritan colony of Massachusetts. The chief characteristic that distin-
       guished the corporate colony from others was the large measure of
       self-government it enjoyed. Qualified voters in the colonies chose the
15   governor, the governor's council, and the legislative assembly.
              Of the thirteen English colonies, seven were founded as
       proprietorships: Maryland, New Hampshire, New Jersey, the Carolinas,
       Pennsylvania, and Georgia. The propriety charters normally granted huge
       tracts of land to an individual, often royalty, or a group of persons on
20   terms similar to feudal tenure. Political control was put in the hands of
       those who received the royal grant, although in most cases it was
       delegated in part to representatives chosen by the colonists.

8. Where in the passage does the author define the commercial joint-stock
    companies?

    (A) Lines 4–7
    (B) Lines 8–10
    (C) Lines 12–14
    (D) Lines 14–15

9. At what point in the passage does the author give the names of the
    colonies established by proprietorship?

    (A) Lines 2–4
    (B) Lines 10–12
    (C) Lines 16–18
    (D) Lines 18–20

10. In which lines does the author explain how the corporate colony was
    different from other colonies?

    (A) Lines 12–14
    (B) Lines 14–15
    (C) Lines 18–20
    (D) Lines 20–22

11. Where in the passage does the author indicate when permanent English settlements were established in North America?

    (A) Lines 1-2
    (B) Lines 2-4
    (C) Lines 4-6
    (D) Lines 10-12

12. In what lines does the author explain proprietorships?

    (A) Lines 12-14
    (B) Lines 16-18
    (C) Lines 18-20
    (D) Lines 20-22

13. Where in the passage does the author discuss the reasons why immigrants came to America?

    (A) Lines 1-2
    (B) Lines 2-4
    (C) Lines 4-7
    (D) Lines 8-10

2 READING FOR REFERENCE AND VOCABULARY

Introducing Reference and Vocabulary
PREREADING QUESTIONS

Answer the following questions.

1. What type of weather predominates in your native country?

2. What kind of weather do you prefer?

3. How do we predict weather today?

Line   Weather is created by the heat of the sun. When the sun shines on the
earth, the air close to the surface heats up, expands, and rises. The higher
it goes, the cooler it becomes. Meanwhile, an area of warmer,
low-pressure air forms below it. Winds are caused by air moving from an
5   area of high pressure to one of low pressure. The closer the pressure
centers are to each other, and the greater the pressure difference between
them, the stronger the wind will be.

     High- and low-pressure air masses travel the globe and cause major
weather changes. When a cold, high-pressure polar air mass meets an
10   extremely low-pressure tropical air mass, their combination can produce
intense storms such as typhoons, hurricanes, and tornadoes. Less severe
weather conditions are often caused by small, local pressure areas. A mild
rainstorm occurs when rising warm air combines with cool air. Clouds are
created as the moist warm air cools and condenses to form water droplets.
15   When clouds reach a saturation point, or the point at which they can no
longer contain their moisture, the droplets fall to earth as rain or snow.

     Weather forecasters look at the movement of warm and cold air
masses and try to predict how they will behave. Although weather
forecasting is not completely accurate, satellites, sophisticated instru-
20   ments, and computers make weather prediction far more accurate today
than in the past. The advantages of weather prediction are numerous, but
in the end, nature does whatever it pleases. We may attempt to predict
weather but we cannot control it.

EXERCISE 1

Answer the following questions.

SKIMMING

1. What is the passage about?

SCANNING

Look over the passage again to find the answers to these questions.

2. What are winds caused by?

3. What causes major weather changes?

4. What happens when rising warm air meets cool air?

5. What do weather forecasters do?

In each of the sentences below, underline the detail that is NOT mentioned in the passage.

6. The passage describes the formation of winds, clouds, rain, and fog.

7. When two opposing pressure systems meet, serious weather conditions such as a typhoon, hurricane, blizzard, or tornado can result.

8. Weather forecasters today use computers, stars, satellites, and special instruments to predict the weather.

REFERENCE QUESTIONS

9. What does "it" in line 4 refer to?

10. What does "them" in line 7 refer to?

11. What does "their" in line 16 refer to?

VOCABULARY QUESTIONS

12. What do you think the word "intense" in line 11 means? Find another word with a similar meaning in the sentences near it.

13. What happens when air "condenses" according to line 14? What do you think "condenses" means here?

14. What does "saturation point" in line 15 mean? Where in the passage is the meaning of the saturation point given?

15. What do you think "sophisticated instruments" in line 19 means? Give two examples of sophisticated instruments that you know.

Reference and Vocabulary Questions

REFERENCE QUESTIONS

Instead of repeating words or phrases, the second time we use them we refer to them by reference words. Reference words are in many cases pronouns such as "it," "them," "they," or "this."

Reference questions ask what certain reference words, such as "they" or "this," refer to. The incorrect answers are other nouns that are mentioned in the passage. To answer a reference question, substitute the four choices given to you for the reference word. The one that is the best substitute for it is the correct answer.

Sample Reading Passage

Line   Although "lie detectors" are being used by governments, police departments, and businesses that all want guaranteed ways of detecting the truth, the results are not always accurate. Lie detectors are properly called emotion detectors, for their aim is to measure bodily changes that
5   contradict what a person says. The polygraph machine records changes in heart rate, breathing, blood pressure, and the electrical activity of the skin (galvanic skin response, or GSR). In the first part of the polygraph test, you are electronically connected to the machine and asked a few neutral questions ("What is your name?" "Where do you live?"). Your physical
10   reactions serve as the standard (baseline) for evaluating what comes next. Then you are asked a few critical questions among the neutral ones ("When did you rob the bank?"). The assumption is that if you are guilty, your body will reveal the truth, even if you try to deny it. Your heart rate, respiration, and GSR will change abruptly as you respond to the
15   incriminating questions.

    That is the theory; but psychologists have found that lie detectors are simply not reliable. Since most physical changes are the same across the emotions, machines cannot tell whether you are feeling guilty, angry, nervous, thrilled, or revved up from an exciting day. Innocent people may

20   be tense and nervous about the whole procedure. They may react
physiologically to a certain word ("bank") not because they robbed it, but
because they recently bounced a check. In either case the machine will
record a "lie." The reverse mistake is also common. Some practiced liars
can lie without flinching, and others learn to beat the machine by tensing
25   muscles or thinking about an exciting experience during neutral
questions.

QUESTION

1. In line 11, the word "ones" refers to

   (A) reactions
   (B) evaluations
   (C) questions
   (D) standards

ANSWER

The best answer is (C); in the context of the passage, "ones" replaces the word
"questions."

QUESTION

1. The word "it" in line 13 refers to

   (A) the question
   (B) the assumption
   (C) the truth
   (D) your body

ANSWER

The best answer is (C); all four choices are synonyms for "critical," but in the
context of the passage only the word "important" can be logically used.

QUESTION

1. In line 12, the word "assumption" could be best replaced with

   (A) statement
   (B) belief
   (C) faith
   (D) imagining

ANSWER

The best answer is (B); answer (A) is not correct because if it were a statement
we do not know who made it. The three other choices are synonyms for
"assumption," but in the context of the passage only the word "belief" can be
logically used.

Strategies for Reference and Vocabulary Questions

- When answering reference questions be aware that the noun closest to the reference word may not always be the correct answer.
- Reference words may refer to a noun or to a noun phrase made up of several words.
- If you do not know which of the four choices is the correct answer to a reference question, substitute the choices for the reference word.
- If you are unable to answer a vocabulary-in-context question, try to guess the meaning from the context by looking for clues.
- Sometimes the meaning of the word is given near the word in the form of a synonym or paraphrase.
- Sometimes clues are not given but are implied. You can guess the meaning after you have read the whole passage.
- The answer choices for the vocabulary-in-context questions may appear correct because they share the literal meaning of the word, but not the meaning as used in the passage. Look for the meaning as it is used in the passage.

Exercises on Reference and Vocabulary

EXERCISE 2

Each item has an underlined word or phrase. From the four choices, (A), (B), (C), and (D), choose the best word or phrase that can be substituted for the underlined word or phrase in its context.

1. A blizzard is a <u>severe</u> winter storm, which occurs in North America.
   - (A) chronic
   - (B) strict
   - (C) painful
   - (D) harsh

2. A musical comedy has a <u>plot</u> with songs and dances connected to it.
   - (A) story
   - (B) plan
   - (C) piece of ground
   - (D) setting

3. Drugs such as tranquilizers, high blood pressure medicines, and steroids are often the culprits of depression.

   (A) crooks
   (B) offenders
   (C) causes
   (D) lawbreakers

4. Industries that work with asbestos and silica have made strides in protecting their workers.

   (A) paces
   (B) improvements
   (C) walks
   (D) movements

5. Lasers can be used to create stunning visual effects.

   (A) shocking
   (B) striking
   (C) handsome
   (D) dazed

6. The olive tree is a hardy shrub that can live for 1,500 years.

   (A) firm
   (B) tough
   (C) seasoned
   (D) fit

7. Wolves live in packs in which there are strong bonds of loyalty.

   (A) securities'
   (B) warranties
   (C) marks
   (D) ties

8. Several developments contributed to the end of the cattle boom.

   (A) bonanza
   (B) panic
   (C) blast
   (D) inflation

9. The stomach breaks down food with digestive juices.

   (A) moisture
   (B) saps
   (C) secretions
   (D) chemicals

10. Influenza is <u>an acute</u> disease of the respiratory tract.
    (A) a sharp
    (B) an important
    (C) a cutting
    (D) a severe

11. Language is an important factor in the <u>accumulation</u> of culture.
    (A) storage
    (B) acquisition
    (C) completion
    (D) control

12. According to the ancient Greeks, the heart was the <u>seat</u> of human intelligence.
    (A) chair
    (B) situation
    (C) center
    (D) place

13. A star starts life as a large ball of rotating gas that slowly <u>contracts</u>.
    (A) catches
    (B) shrinks
    (C) deflates
    (D) agrees

14. American immigration in the nineteenth century <u>peaked</u> in the 1880s.
    (A) was pointed
    (B) was topped
    (C) was at its highest point
    (D) was sharp

Note: For more vocabulary-in-context practice see Peterson's *TOEFL® Word Flash*.

Exercise 3

> **Read the following passages and answer the reference questions that follow each one.**

QUESTIONS 1–5

Line George Lucas's Star Wars changed the direction of American film with
some of the most ingenious special effects contrived for movies of its time.
Twenty-two months were spent on the special effects, including the six
months needed to design the equipment and the more than 1,000 story
5   boards for the effects sequences.

A special computerized camera, called a Dykstraflex, was designed
to give the illusion of real screen movement. This system, controlled by
the camera operator, enabled him or her to pan, tilt, and track around the
model, always keeping it in focus. The breakthrough was the camera's
10   ability to repeat the identical movements from shot to shot; thus the
effects sequences could be built like a music track; layer upon layer. The
illusion was complete: none of the spaceships in Star Wars ever
moved–only the camera did.

The star-field backdrop in space was made by punching holes in
15   black plexiglass. More than 75 models were constructed, with astonishing
detail work. On the rebel blockade runner artists built a tiny cockpit, all
done to scale. The miniaturized laser canons were fully motorized to
swivel and tilt by remote control. The light sabers were four-sided blades
coated with reflective aluminum, attached to a small motor. When rotated,
20   they created a flashing light later enhanced by animation.

1. The word "some" in line 2 refers to
   (A) American film
   (B) direction
   (C) movies
   (D) special effects

2. In line 2, the word "contrived" could be best replaced with which of
   the following?
   (A) Discovered
   (B) Created
   (C) Performed
   (D) Utilized

3. In line 7, "this system" refers to

   (A) the creation of an illusion
   (B) screen movement
   (C) panning and tilting around a model
   (D) a special computerized camera

4. The word "it" in line 9 refers to the

   (A) model
   (B) camera
   (C) focus
   (D) system

5. The word "they" in line 20 refers to the

   (A) miniaturized laser cannons
   (B) artists
   (C) four-sided blades
   (D) seventy-five models

QUESTIONS 6–10

Line   There are three main types of sedimentary rocks, which are classified
according to the origin and size of their particles. One type, called
evaporites, is formed from chemically derived sediments. For example, an
inland sea might evaporate and leave a deposit of rock salt.

5   The second type is derived entirely from organic material. Since it is
a fossil in its own right, it is called fossiliferous rock. Fossiliferous rocks,
such as limestones and chalks, are formed from calcium-based skeletons of
tiny organisms deposited on the seabed. Some limestones are fossilized
corals; others, known as tufa, are derived from mosses and other plants

10   that grow beside hot springs. Carbon-based rocks, such as coal and jet, are
the remains of plant material laid down in huge quantities. The remains of
sponges and microscopic diatoms constitute rocks such as chert and flint.

           The third type of sedimentary rock is clastic. It is formed from
eroded particles of other rocks and is graded according to the size of these

15   particles. Fine shales are perhaps the most significant sedimentary rocks
covering the earth.

           The sedimentary rocks most likely to contain fossils are those that
were laid down in places where there was abundant life and where
disposition was rapid enough to bury the organisms before their bodies

20   were broken up and decomposed. The sandy bottoms of shallow, calm
seas, river deltas, lagoons, and deserts are the most likely places to give
rise to fossils. The finer the sediment, the finer the detail recorded in
them. Details such as the fur of those reptilian flyers, the pterosaurs, are
only visible because they were fossilized in exceptionally fine limestone.

6. In line 2 the word "their" refers to

   (A) particles
   (B) sedimentary rocks
   (C) origin and size
   (D) classification

7. As used in this passage, the word "material" refers to

   (A) cloth
   (B) articles
   (C) matter
   (D) values

8. The word "others" in line 9 refers to

   (A) fossilized corals
   (B) limestones
   (C) tiny organisms
   (D) mosses

9. To which of the following does the word "those" in line 17 refer?

   (A) Sedimentary rocks
   (B) Fossils
   (C) Organisms
   (D) Fine shales

10. The word "them" in line 23 refers to

    (A) sediments
    (B) fossils
    (C) details
    (D) limestones

QUESTIONS 11–15

Line On a drop shot, a tennis player "drops" the ball just over the net, hoping that his or her opponent won't get to it at all or will just barely reach it, thus making a weak return. The drop shot works well in a number of situations. It can be used to tire an opponent, to bring a baseline player to
5   the net, to win points outright when an opponent is slow in moving forward or is out of position, or to substitute for the approach shot.

A perfect situation for a drop shot occurs when a player's opponent is far out of court and hits well to the inside of the service line. A good drop shot is a sure winner, but a bad one is equally certain disaster. The
10 opponent who gets to the ball early has been handed the net position, which is a distinct advantage for the net rusher who will usually win the point in short order.

There are two types of drop shots, each requiring a distinct stroke.
The first is used to drop slow balls descending from the peak of the
15 bounce. The second is used on rising balls. These shots require excellent
timing and a simple stroke, such as the swing on waist-high volleys.

11. The word "it" in line 2 refers to

    (A) his or her opponent
    (B) the ball
    (C) the net
    (D) a weak return

12. In line 9, the word "one" refers to

    (A) a disaster
    (B) a sure winner
    (C) the service line
    (D) a drop shot

13. The word "who" in line 10 refers to

    (A) the net rusher
    (B) the net position
    (C) the advantage
    (D) the opponent

14. In line 11 the word "which" refers to

    (A) the opponent
    (B) a distinct advantage
    (C) the net position
    (D) the winning point

15. The word "distinct" in line 11 is closest in meaning to which of the
    following?

    (A) Difficult
    (B) Comparable
    (C) Definite
    (D) Practiced

QUESTIONS 16–20
Line Every year in late December, a southward-moving current warms the
water along the Pacific coast of Peru. Because the warm current arrives
around Christmas, the Peruvians named it El Nino, "boychild." Until the
mid-1970s, El Nino was an unrecognized local phenomenon, until
5 scientists began to realize that El Nino, later named El Nino Southern
Oscillation (ENSO), is part of a huge ocean and atmosphere that is felt as
far away as Australia and Indonesia.

Every few years the El Nino current is warmer than normal, causing
greater ocean warming and consequently changes in the normal patterns

10 of sea and surface temperatures. The resulting changes in atmospheric
pressure affect trade speeds and the location of the largest thunderstorms,
thus affecting weather patterns around the world. The shift in location of
the Pacific's largest thunderstorms, which usually occur from the Western
Pacific to the Central Pacific, changes global weather patterns because the
15 thunderstorms pump air into the atmosphere in different places than
normal. The result is a shift in the location of high- and low-pressure areas,
wind patterns, and the paths followed by storms.

From 1982 to 1983 the El Nino condition caused greater than
average precipitation along the U.S. West Coast and sent five hurricanes to
20 French Polynesia, which normally goes years without hurricanes. That
same year, El Nino was linked to floods in Louisiana, Florida, Cuba,
Ecuador, Peru, and Bolivia, and to droughts in Hawaii, Mexico, Southern
Africa, the Philippines, Indonesia, and Australia.

In response to the 1982–83 global weather disruption, the World
25 Meteorological Organization initiated the Tropical Ocean and Global
Atmosphere (TOGA) program. The goal of the ten-year program is to gain
understanding of El Nino so scientists can forecast future El Nino episodes
and their likely results.

16. In line 3 the word "it" refers to

(A) December
(B) the warm current
(C) Christmas
(D) the coast of Peru

17. To what does the word "that" in line 6 refer?

(A) A local phenomenon
(B) An ocean and atmosphere system
(C) The El Nino Southern Oscillation
(D) Scientists

18. In line 13 the word "which" refers to

(A) shifts in location
(B) global weather patterns
(C) the atmosphere
(D) thunderstorms

19. In line 25 the word "initiated" could best be replaced with which of the
following?

(A) Produced
(B) Established
(C) Disrupted
(D) Responded to

20. The word "their" in line 28 refers to
    - **(A)** scientists
    - **(B)** future events
    - **(C)** El Nino episodes
    - **(D)** results

QUESTIONS 21–25

Line   There are about two dozen species of seahorses, all of which are aquatic. Their tails are prehensile and very agile, but do not propel them fast enough to catch the living food they need. Therefore, seahorses have evolved another method of catching their prey. They use extremely strong
5   suction that whips animals such as brine shrimp into their open mouths. Seahorses have eyes that move independently of each other, which enable them to spot potential food, and predators, more easily. The seahorse's genus name is *Hippocampus*, which translates as "horse catepillar."

21. The word "they" in line 3 refers to
    - **(A)** the tails of seahorses
    - **(B)** aquatic animals
    - **(C)** sources of food
    - **(D)** species of seahorses

22. As used in line 4 the word "evolved" means
    - **(A)** grown
    - **(B)** developed
    - **(C)** produced
    - **(D)** changed

23. The word "they" in line 4 refers to
    - **(A)** prehensile tails
    - **(B)** prey
    - **(C)** seahorses
    - **(D)** methods

24. In line 7, the word "them" refers to
    - **(A)** eyes
    - **(B)** predators
    - **(C)** seahorses
    - **(D)** brine shrimp

25. In line 8 the word "which" refers to
    - **(A)** potential food
    - **(B)** *Hippocampus*
    - **(C)** horse caterpillar
    - **(D)** a translation

QUESTIONS 26–30

Line   Planes are subjected to drag forces because an object moving forward
through the air is hampered by it to a greater or lesser extent, since the air
or any gas has friction. A plane in subsonic flight is preceded by the
pressure waves it creates as it makes its way through the air. These pressure
5   waves push away the air in front of the plane so there is less drag than
would otherwise be the case. But when a plane reaches sonic speed, or the
speed of sound, the pressure waves no longer precede the plane. They no
longer push away any of the air in front of the craft, so the drag forces
become much greater. The large rise in drag as the plane approaches Mach
10   1, or the speed of sound, is referred to as the sonic barrier.
        Even a conventional subsonic plane traveling at a speed below Mach
1 can encounter an extreme rise in drag. This is because the pressure over
the wing is decreased as the wing moves through the air. This results from
the increase in the speed of the air stream over the wing in accordance
15   with the law of physics called *Bernoulli's principle*.

26. The word "subjected" in line 1 is closest in meaning to which of the
    following?

    (A) Affected
    (B) Hampered
    (C) Confronted
    (D) Exposed

27. In line 2 the word "it" refers to

    (A) drag force
    (B) an object
    (C) the air
    (D) a plane

28. The word "it" in line 4 refers to

    (A) a plane in subsonic flight
    (B) a pressure wave
    (C) air or any gas
    (D) drag force

29. In line 7, the word "they" refers to

    (A) planes reaching sonic speed
    (B) pressure waves
    (C) drag forces
    (D) conventional subsonic planes

30. To which of the following does the word "this" in line 12 refer?

    (A) A decrease in pressure over the wing
    (B) An increase in the speed of the air stream over the wing
    (C) Pressure waves preceding the plane
    (D) A rise in drag encountered by a subsonic plane

CHAPTER 3

READING FOR MAIN IDEAS

Introducing Main Ideas
PREREADING QUESTIONS

Answer the following questions.

1. Why do you think people exercise?
2. What things should you do to be healthy?
3. What foods should you eat to be healthy?

Line   A healthful lifestyle leads to a longer, happier, healthier life. Staying healthy means eating a well-balanced diet, getting regular exercise, and avoiding things that are bad for the body and mind.

5   Nutrition plays a key role in maintaining good health and preventing many diseases. In spite of all the information available about diets, scientists still believe that good nutrition can be simple. There are several basic rules to follow. Keep fat intake low. Eat foods high in carbohydrates, which are the starches in grains, legumes (beans and peas), vegetables, and some fruits. Avoid too much sugar. Limit salt. Eat lots of fruits and

10   vegetables, which are high in vitamins.

A healthful lifestyle in an active lifestyle. Lack of proper physical exercise can cause tiredness, irritability, and poor general health. Physical fitness requires both aerobic exercise, such as running, bicycle riding, and swimming, and muscle-strengthening exercises, such as weight lifting.

15   Finally, good health is acquired by saying no to bad habits such as smoking, drinking, and overeating and by avoiding situations that are constantly stressful. People can take their lives and happiness into their own hands. Maintaining a healthy lifestyle is the first step.

Exercise 1

Answer the following questions.

SKIMMING

Skim or read the passage over quickly. Do not read each detail carefully. Usually, but not always, the main idea is found in the first sentence of a paragraph.

Underline the main idea in paragraph 2.
Underline the main idea in paragraph 3.
Underline the main idea in paragraph 4.

1. What is the main idea of the whole passage?

SCANNING

Look over the passage again to find the answers to questions 2–12. Complete the following sentences with details from the passage.

2. Three kinds of food that you should avoid having too much of are
   _____, _____, and _____.

3. Three problems that lack of physical exercise can cause are
   _____, _____, and _____.

4. Two kinds of aerobic exercise mentioned in the passage are
   _____ and _____.

5. Grains, legumes, vegetables, and some fruits all contain _____.

6. Fruits and vegetables contain a lot of _____.

In each of the sentences below, underline the detail that is NOT mentioned in the passage.

7. Smoking, drinking, excessive eating, dieting, and stressful situations are not good for your health.

8. Physical fitness for a healthy lifestyle includes regular walking, aerobic exercise, and muscle-strengthening exercises.

REFERENCE AND VOCABULARY QUESTIONS.

9. What does the word "their" in its second appearance on line 17 refer to?

10. What does the word "nutrition" in line 4 mean?

11. What would be the best substitute for the word "limit" in line 9?

12. What does the word "constantly" in line 17 mean?

Main Idea Questions

One of the most frequently asked questions in the Reading Comprehension section is about the main idea of the passage. There is usually one such question for each reading passage. As its name suggests, the main idea is the most important idea in the passage or what the passage is about. Each passage has main and subordinate, or less important, ideas. The main idea is more general than the supporting ideas or details in the passage. The main idea may be the first sentence in the paragraph, but this is not always the case. The main idea may appear in the middle or toward the end.

When the main idea of a passage is not clear because each paragraph has a different main point, a question identifying the main topic of the passage will be asked. The following are examples of main idea questions:

What is the main idea of the passage?
What is the main idea expressed in the passage?
What does the passage mainly discuss?
With what topic is the passage mainly concerned?
The primary idea of the passage is . . .
The main topic of the passage is . . .

If the main idea of the passage is not clear because each paragraph has a different main point, then summarize or combine the main points of each paragraph to find the main idea. The main idea should relate to the entire passage and not to just one part of it. Also, the main idea should not be so general that it goes beyond the passage.

The four answer choices to the main idea questions will contain the following types of answers:

(A) Too general
(B) True but only a detail
(C) Incorrect
(D) Correct

Sample Reading Passage

Line Although "lie detectors" are being used by governments, police departments, and businesses that all want guaranteed ways of detecting the truth, the results are not always accurate. Lie detectors are properly called emotion detectors, for their aim is to measure bodily changes that
5 contradict what a person says. The polygraph machine records changes in heart rate, breathing, blood pressure, and the electrical activity of the skin (galvanic skin response, or GSR). In the first part of the polygraph test, you are electronically connected to the machine and asked a few neutral questions ("What is your name?" "Where do you live?"). Your physical
10 reactions serve as the standard (baseline) for evaluating what comes next. Then you are asked a few critical questions among the neutral ones ("When did you rob the bank?"). The assumption is that if you are guilty,

your body will reveal the truth, even if you try to deny it. Your heart rate, respiration, and GSR will change abruptly as you respond to the
15   incriminating questions.

That is the theory; but psychologists have found that lie detectors are simply not reliable. Since most physical changes are the same across the emotions, machines cannot tell whether you are feeling guilty, angry, nervous, thrilled, or revved up from an exciting day. Innocent people may
20   be tense and nervous about the whole procedure. They may react physiologically to a certain word ("bank") not because they robbed it, but because they recently bounced a check. In either case the machine will record a "lie." The reverse mistake is also common. Some practiced liars can lie without flinching, and others learn to beat the machine by tensing
25   muscles or thinking about an exciting experience during neutral questions.

QUESTION

1. What is the main idea of the passage?

    (A) Physical reactions reveal guilt.
    (B) How lie detectors are used and their reliability.
    (C) Lie detectors distinguish different emotions.
    (D) Lie detectors make innocent people nervous.

ANSWER

Answer (A) is not correct because it is too general and does not have anything to do with lie detectors. Answer (C) is incorrect because lie detectors record only physical changes in the body and not emotions. A lie detector cannot determine whether you are angry or nervous. Answer (D) is incorrect because although lie detectors make innocent people nervous, this is only a detail and not the main point. The best answer is (B) since this combines the main point of the first paragraph, which is about the use of the lie detector, with the main point of the second paragraph, which is about the reliability of the lie detector.

Exercises on Main Ideas

EXERCISE 2

> **Read the following passages and find the main idea of each one.**

Strictly speaking, cartography is the drawing or compiling of maps. The explorers and surveyors go out and make the measurements and gather the information from which the cartographers draw their maps. Sometimes the fieldwork and the creation of the map are done by the same person. But when the scope is broad and the sources of information many, maps are more often a compilation of that information. They represent the accumulated work of many people, brought together under the supervision of one person, the compiler. The value of the map depends, of course, on the expertise of the compiler, who must sift through available information, select the most accurate data, and come up with a thoughtful and accurate synthesis of the geographic knowledge of the region.

Strategies

- The main idea is not always the first sentence in the paragraph or passage. It can also appear in the middle or toward the end of a paragraph.
- When the main idea is not clear because each paragraph has a main point, combine all the main points to get the main idea.
- Make sure the answer you select for the main idea question relates to the whole passage and not just to one part of it. You can scan the passage to see whether the main idea you have selected is discussed all through the passage.
- The wrong choices for main idea questions may be one of the following:

1. True statements that focus on one paragraph or a detail

2. Statements that are too general and go beyond the passage

3. Statements that are incorrect misinterpretations of the main idea

Or, briefly:

   1. Too specific
   2. Too general
   3. Incorrect

1. What is the main idea of the passage?

   (A) The definition of cartography is the drawing or compiling of maps.
   (B) Maps are the product of a group effort brought together usually by one person.
   (C) Not all of the information initially compiled for maps is accurate.
   (D) The compiler's task is more important than that of the explorers and surveyors.

In the 1820s and 1830s American painting added a new chapter to the story of its development. Until the nineteenth century, portraiture and occasional historical pieces were the only concerns of American art, but throughout the 1800s some of America's most talented painters chose to depict landscapes and the daily activities of ordinary people. With the nation's declaration of independence had come prosperity and with it the opportunity and inclination for painters to contemplate their environment. As they traveled beyond the early settlements and left the nation's first cities, such as Boston and Philadelphia, they began to experience and appreciate the pristine beauty of the American scenery, which differed greatly from the European landscape, partly because in its unsettled state it appeared wild and primeval.

2. What is the main topic of the passage?

   (A) Conditions in the early 1800s were favorable to the emergence of the American landscape artist.
   (B) In the early 1800s, landscapes were produced in preference to portraits and historical pieces.
   (C) America's declaration of independence brought prosperity to the nation and with it an appreciation of the outdoors.
   (D) An increase in travel in America led to an appreciation of the beauty of the American landscape.

Speculation about the earth's crust has a special edge of urgency in California, which sits on the San Andreas fault, the world's most famous and respected fracture zone. Not surprisingly, it was a scientist at the California Institute of Technology, Charles F. Richter, who invented the Richter scale used to measure earthquakes. Seismic activity in California is being constantly monitored and mapped. Seismometers register many thousands of small earthquakes every year, and computers instantly calculate the location, depth, and magnitude of an earthquake. Laser distance-ranging networks can detect changes of length, indicating change in crustal stress, accurate to about half an inch in 20 miles. Satellite measurements of crustal blocks are improving, and California seismologists believe they may in time be precise enough to allow earthquake prediction.

3. What is the main idea expressed in the passage?

(A) The Richter scale was invented in California.
(B) Computers provide a variety of information about earthquakes.
(C) A great deal of attention is paid to earthquake activity in California.
(D) Earthquake prediction will be possible in the future.

The first expedition down the Colorado River was made by John Wesley Powell and his party in 1869. Powell had made long trips down the Ohio and the Mississippi and its tributaries during his twenties, when his lifelong interest in natural history developed. In 1867 he led his first expedition to the Rockies, a collecting trip for the museum he had founded in Illinois. While on Pike's Peak, near Colorado Springs, Powell conceived his great plan to explore the Colorado River. On May 24, 1869, he and his party set off down the upper Colorado and nothing was heard from them for thirty-seven days. During that time Powell and party braved uncharted territory, encounters with the natives, fierce rapids, and 20-foot waterfalls, as they followed the Colorado through the Grand Canyon to the Gulf of California.

4. What is the main subject of the passage?

(A) Powell was uniquely qualified to lead an expedition down the Colorado.
(B) Powell was inspired to explore the Colorado while on Pike's Peak.
(C) People were concerned when nothing was heard from Powell and his party for over a month.
(D) Powell and his party faced daunting challenges on the first Colorado River expedition.

Innovations in transportation in the 1800s permitted space to be traversed more rapidly and were crucial to the industrial expansion of the North. The great spaces that separated producers from consumers made speed essential, especially in the movement of perishable freight. The development of the steam-powered locomotive in the 1830s and the rapid extension of the railways in the 1840s and 1850s provided the answer to the need for faster transport and dramatically altered patterns of economic development throughout the United States. In 1830 there were 32 miles of rails in the country, in 1840 there were 2,818 miles, and by 1850 there were more than 9,000 miles. The rapid extension of rail mileage enabled the railroads significantly to reduce their costs for shipping freight and carrying passengers, thus enabling them to price their services more cheaply and competitively. The extension of trunk lines, into which short or local lines fed, further tightened the east-west flow of commerce and bound the Northeast and the old Northwest together with bands of steel.

5. What is the main theme in the passage?

   (A) Railroad made the transportation of perishable freight possible.
   (B) Between 1830 and 1850 over 8,000 miles of railroad track were laid.
   (C) Railroads provided an important link between the Northwest and the Northeast.
   (D) Railroads had a profound effect on the economic development of the United States in the nineteenth century.

The few places left on earth that have not been altered by humankind are almost invariably hostile to humans. One such place is the Alaskan Arctic, which is inhabited, where inhabited at all, by only a scattering of Eskimos, Native Americans, and whites. But while the Arctic is indeed a chill and inimical realm of snow, ice, and polar bears, it is also a region of great beauty and, above all, purity, where plants and animals still exist undisturbed in a state of natural balance. Nearly one third of Alaska lies north of the Arctic Circle and consists of pristine land. The Brooks Range cuts across the region like a wall, making access difficult. Even today, in an age of jet travel, the number of persons who have had firsthand experience in the Alaskan Arctic remains small, and countless valleys and mountains go unnamed and even unexplored.

6. What is the primary topic of the passage?

   (A) The Alaskan Arctic is a beautifully pristine realm of snow, ice, and polar bears.
   (B) The Alaskan Arctic is habitable only to arctic animals and a few hardy humans.
   (C) The ruggedness of the Alaskan Arctic makes it one of the last few remaining pristine areas in the world.
   (D) Remarkably, parts of the Alaskan Arctic still remain unexplored.

In the first half of the nineteenth century, the first distinctly American culture took form. The rise of an American tradition in literature paralleled the expansion of the nation, as American writers began to look within themselves and across their enlarged continental homeland for their subjects and themes. The romance, or novel, provided a useful form for dealing with the large moral subjects and the peculiar circumstances of the American setting. In James Fenimore Cooper's *The Pioneers* (1823) and *The Deerslayer* (1841), Natty Bumppo and the Mohican guide Chingachgook confronted the environment of the American frontier, chronicling the advance of "civilization" and questioning the implications of its impact on the natural world. The theme of the individual confronting nature was further developed by Herman Melville in the classic novel *Moby Dick* (1951). Nathaniel Hawthorne dealt with equally difficult questions of inner limits and the individual's responsibilities to society in *The Scarlet Letter* (1850) and *The House of the Seven Gables* (1851).

7. What is the main idea expressed in the passage?

   (A) As the nation expanded, novelists began writing about the American frontier.
   (B) The first American literature took the form of novels that dealt with uniquely American themes.
   (C) In their novels, Melville and Hawthorne both addressed difficult questions facing Americans.
   (D) The individual versus nature was one of the main themes explored in early American literature.

Because different tree species adapted to different climates and soil types have evolved over millennia, many kinds of forests occupy the earth today. The primitive forests of several hundred million years ago consisted of fewer kinds of trees. In fact, the earliest "trees," which grew nearly 500 million years ago, were like giant club mosses. They lacked true roots and consisted of a tangle of specialized branches that clambered over rocky ground. Fifty million years later came the dense forests of tree ferns that prevailed in tropical climates of that era. The forerunners of modern conifers were on the scene 300 million years ago, when plant life abundantly colonized marshy land, building the tremendous coal and oil reserves so important today. By the time the dinosaurs roamed the earth some 180 million years ago, during the Cretaceous period, seed-bearing trees had evolved that shed their leaves in winter; from these have sprung the angiosperms and our present deciduous forests.

8. What is the main idea of the passage?

   (A) Conifers are the oldest trees in today's forests.
   (B) Climate affected the development of trees over millennia.
   (C) The predecessors of today's forests were giant club mosses and tree ferns.
   (D) The variety of trees in today's forest are a result of millions of years of evolution.

Birds have two basic types of sounds: songs and calls. Songs are usually more complex than calls and are utilized primarily by adult males during the breeding season to establish territories or attract mates. Calls are normally simple notes, single or repeated, vocalized by males and females in all seasons to express alarm or maintain contact with mates, offspring, or other birds of the same species. All songs and most calls are distinctive, and with concentrated study and practice, bird-watchers can learn to identify many birds by their sounds and to call them as well.

9. What is the main idea of the passage?

(A) Bird calls and songs are distinctive, meaningful, and identifiable.
(B) Bird songs are complicated and used mainly by males to attract mates.
(C) Birds have their own language by which they maintain contact.
(D) Bird-watchers can identify many bird calls and their meanings and learn to mimic them as well.

Hawaii was originally settled by the natives of the South Pacific, who arrived in the islands in canoes laden with breadfruit, yams, taro, coconut, bananas, pigs, and chickens. Supplementing these foods were over a hundred different edible fishes and forty kinds of seaweed from the surrounding waters. Hawaiian food was eaten raw or wrapped in taro leaves, seasoned with coconut, and cooked.

In the early 1800s, the whalers and missionaries introduced stews, chowders, curries, corned beef, dried beef, salt salmon, and Indian and cornstarch puddings. Most likely, pipkaula (jerked beef), lomi lomi salmon, and haupia (coconut pudding) evolved during this period.

In the late nineteenth century immigrants from China, Japan, and Korea were brought to Hawaii to work the sugar plantations. The Chinese brought rice, soybeans, and vegetables and their ways of cooking them. The Japanese brought sukiyaki and teriyaki, among many other foods. Settlers from the continental United States also brought their favorite recipes and in the spirit of aloha, the Hawaiians have accepted each group's offerings and drawn the best from them. Thus a Hawaiian feast is a gastronomic experience, the essence of Hawaii and its many cultures.

10. What is the main topic of the passage?

(A) Whalers and missionaries introduced new kinds of foods to the people of Hawaii.
(B) Sugar plantations were worked by immigrants from Asia, who brought their native foods with them.
(C) Hawaiian food is a combination of the foods of many peoples and a reflection of Hawaii's history.
(D) The natives of the South Pacific who first settled in Hawaii ate raw food, whereas other immigrants cooked theirs.

CHAPTER 4

READING FOR INFERENCE

Introducing Inference
PREREADING QUESTIONS

Answer the following questions.

1. What do you think motion pictures were like ninety years ago?

2. What are some uses for motion pictures?

3. What are your favorite kinds of movies?

Line When people think of movies, they usually think of Hollywood. However, many of the earliest tools relating to motion pictures were not American inventions. It was thanks to the efforts of inventors from several countries that we can enjoy movies today.

5   In the early 1800s an Englishman named William George Horner invented the zoetrope. In it a series of pictures were mounted inside a drum. When the rotating pictures were viewed through slots, they merged into one and appeared to move. In California in 1877, another Englishman, named Eadweard Muybridge, used a series of cameras to record the

10 movements of a galloping horse. Later, he also recorded human movements. He used his still pictures to illustrate books; thus it was left to the German, Ottomar Anschutz, to invent a way to rapidly show the picture series to give the impression of movement. Finally, it took a Frenchman, Etienne-Jules Marey, to develop a single camera to record

15 movement. Marey shot his pictures on fixed plates, at the rate of 12 per second. As early as 1888 he was experimenting with celluloid film, an American invention.

     While Thomas Edison was busy inventing something called the kinetograph camera, Louis Le Prince of France was patenting a 16-lens

20 camera to take moving pictures and a projector to show them. By the following year he was working with a single-lens camera. Unfortunately, in 1890 Le Prince suddenly disappeared from the train in which he was traveling and vanished forever. Taking up where Le Prince left off were Louis and Auguste Lumiere, who gave the world's first projected film

25 performance, before a paying audience in Paris on December 28, 1895.

48

Motion pictures have come a long way since those early days and have had a great influence on society. It was thanks to the contributions of filmmakers and inventors from all over the world that movies have developed into the form we know today.

EXERCISE 1

Answer the following questions.

SKIMMING
Read the passage over quickly.

1. What is the main idea of the passage?

SCANNING
Look over the passage again to find the answers to questions 2–12. Complete the following sentences with details from the passage.

2. A _____ was an invention that consisted of a drum with a series of pictures that rotated and were viewed through slots.

3. After Muybridge recorded the movements of a galloping horse, he recorded _____.

4. Marey was the first person to use one _____ to record movement.

5. Marey experimented with _____, which he did not invent.

6. The first projected film performance was given by the _____ brothers.

In each of the sentences below, underline the detail that is NOT mentioned the passage.

7. Muybridge used a series of cameras to record the movements of a galloping horse, human movements, and the movement of objects.

8. At the same time Thomas Edison invented and patented the kinetograph camera, Le Prince patented a 16-lens camera to take moving pictures.

REFERENCE AND VOCABULARY QUESTIONS

9. What does the word "it" in line 6 refer to?

10. What does the word "they" in line 7 refer to?

11. What do you think the word "merged" in line 7 means?

12. What does the word "contributions" in line 27 mean?

INFERENCE

The answers to these questions are not directly stated in the passage, but are understood by drawing conclusions from the information given in the passage.

13. What do you think would have happened if Le Prince had not disappeared?

14. What can we infer about the motion picture camera from the passage?

Inference Questions

Inference questions are perhaps the most difficult questions to answer in the Reading Comprehension section. The answers to these questions are not directly stated in the passage but are understood, or implied. The following are examples of inference questions:

Which of the following can be inferred about . . . ?
Which of the following can be inferred from the passage?
From the passage, it can be inferred that . . . .
The passage implies that . . . .
The author implies that . . . .
The passage suggests that . . . .
It is most probable that . . . .

To answer inference questions, you must decide what logical conclusion follows from the facts stated in the passage. These ideas may be what the author believes to be true but has not stated in the passage.

EXAMPLE

Lie detectors are properly called emotion detectors, for their aim is to measure bodily changes that contradict what a person says.

What can be inferred from the sentence?

• Lie detectors record a person's emotions.
• Emotions can contradict what a person says.

What cannot be inferred from the sentence?

• People always say what they are feeling. (Bodily changes can contradict what a person says.)
• Lie detectors cause changes in emotions. (No. Lie detectors measure or record bodily changes.)

Sample Reading Passage

Line   Although "lie detectors" are being used by governments, police departments, and businesses that all want guaranteed ways of detecting the truth, the results are not always accurate. Lie detectors are properly called emotion detectors, for their aim is to measure bodily changes that

5   contradict what a person says. The polygraph machine records changes in heart rate, breathing, blood pressure, and the electrical activity of the skin (galvanic skin response, or GSR). In the first part of the polygraph test, you are electronically connected to the machine and asked a few neutral questions ("What is your name?" "Where do you live?"). Your physical

10   reactions serve as the standard (baseline) for evaluating what comes next. Then you are asked a few critical questions among the neutral ones ("When did you rob the bank?"). The assumption is that if you are guilty, your body will reveal the truth, even if you try to deny it. Your heart rate, respiration, and GSR will change abruptly as you respond to the

15   incriminating questions.

        That is the theory; but psychologists have found that lie detectors are simply not reliable. Since most physical changes are the same across the emotions, machines cannot tell whether you are feeling guilty, angry, nervous, thrilled, or revved up from an exciting day. Innocent people may

20   be tense and nervous about the whole procedure. They may react physiologically to a certain word ("bank") not because they robbed it, but because they recently bounced a check. In either case the machine will record a "lie." The reverse mistake is also common. Some practiced liars can lie without flinching, and others learn to beat the machine by tensing

25   muscles or thinking about an exciting experience during neutral questions.

QUESTION

1. Which of the following can be inferred from the passage?

    (A) Lie detectors are very reliable.
    (B) Innocent people are never found guilty.
    (C) Psychologists never argue about anything.
    (D) Most people cannot control their bodily reactions.

ANSWER

Answer (A) is incorrect because the second paragraph states that psychologists find lie detectors to be unreliable. Answer (B) is also incorrect, because the passage states that the lie detector may record innocent people as lying in response to a question, not because they are guilty but because they are nervous. Therefore, innocent people may be found guilty. Answer (C) is also incorrect, because although psychologists may agree on the unreliability of lie detectors, we do not know whether they agree on other issues. Therefore, this cannot be inferred. Answer (D) is the best answer. Although we know that some practiced liars can control their bodily reactions, in general, we can infer that most people cannot control their bodily reactions such as breathing rate, heart rate, blood pressure, and the electrical activity of the skin.

QUESTION

1. From the passage, it can be inferred that
   (A) Emotions are all the same.
   (B) Psychologists would not want the detectors used to prove some-one's guilt.
   (C) Neutral questions reveal the truth.
   (D) Psychologists are unreliable.

ANSWER

Answer (A) cannot be inferred. The passage states that physical changes are the same across all emotions, but that does not mean that emotions are all the same. Answer (C) also cannot be inferred since the passage states that some practiced liars can beat the machine. Answer (D) cannot be inferred since the passage states that psychologists find the detectors unreliable; there is no indication in the passage that psychologists are unreliable. The best answer is (B) since it can be inferred that psychologists would not want to use lie detectors to prove someone's guilt, because they consider them to be unreliable.

Strategies

- Go beyond the information stated in the passage.
- Draw a conclusion or reason out what is implied—that is, what the author of the passage means or believes to be true but has not stated in the passage.
- Remember that the answer to the question will not be stated in words in the passage.
- Beware of answer choices that go beyond what you can logically infer from the passage. Wrong answer choices will often be too exaggerated or overstated to be precisely correct.

Exercises on Inference

EXERCISE 2

> Read the following passages and the statements that follow
> them. Some statements can be inferred from the passages,
> others cannot. Put a check mark next to the statements that
> can be inferred from the passages.

QUESTIONS 1–7

The mid-1950s saw the growth of a new kind of popular music that was first called "rock 'n' roll" and then simply "rock." Although quite diverse in style, rock music tends to be vocal music with a hard, driving beat often featuring electric guitar accompaniment and heavily amplified sound. Early rock grew mainly out of rhythm and blues, a dance music of African Americans that combined blues, jazz, and gospel styles. Rock also drew upon country and western music, a folklike guitar-based style associated with rural Americans and the Nashville Grand Ole Opry. In little more than a decade, rock evolved from a single, dance-oriented style to a music highly varied in its tones, lyrics, and electronic technology.

_____ 1. Rock was the first form of popular music.

_____ 2. There is basically one style of rock music.

_____ 3. Rock music is often loud.

_____ 4. Several types of music influenced the development of rock.

_____ 5. Rock has always been a complicated style of music.

_____ 6. Folk music is popular in rural areas.

_____ 7. The evolution of rock music occurred relatively quickly.

QUESTIONS 8–13

Immigrants from Europe brought their customs and outlooks to the new and often harsh environments in the New World. To survive, they had to adjust to the new conditions of life in the American colonies, enforced by nature and by the British government. To prosper, they had to overcome great odds: the sheer distance between the settlers, a constant scarcity of labor, and the lack of liquid capital and a circulating currency.

In the middle and northern colonies, these conditions inspired diversity and innovation. Severe winters and poor soil largely determined the economy of the New England colonies, which relied on trading and the sea for their economic development. Along the New England coast, industries related to seafaring and shipbuilding developed. The middle colonies possessed good soil and a moderate climate, so they developed staple crop agriculture and related industries, such as flour mills. Craftsmen and artisans were also attracted to these areas and set up mills to produce textiles, paper, glass, and iron. In the South the prospects of great wealth from large-scale crop agriculture led farmers to establish plantations given to the production of a single cash crop, such as tobacco or cotton.

_____ 8. The early immigrants had to learn to adapt their old ways of doing things to a new environment.

_____ 9. There was more work in the colonies than people to do it.

_____10. The hardships faced by the colonists hindered them from being inventive.

_____11. The geographic location of the colonies influenced their economic development.

_____12. Farming often hampered the economic development of communities in the colonies.

_____13. It was by sheer luck that certain colonies prospered.

QUESTIONS 14–20

Professional photographers have been engaged in a contest with nature since the origin of their craft. They have ventured into the most adverse conditions, from the broiling heat and stinging sand of the Sahara to the extreme cold of the Arctic, to capture the perfect image. Although setting, lighting, and action all pose challenges to the photographer, environmental obstacles are in many ways the trickiest to surmount. Heat, humidity, dust, and cold all jeopardize photographic materials and equipment. The harm caused by these conditions is sometimes immediately obvious, such as when the shutter or film-advance mechanism jams, but often it is impossible to detect until after the film is developed or the effects of camera corrosion show up.

To avoid catastrophes, photographers have devised a number of ingenious ways to protect their equipment, from sophisticated cases and housings to simple plastic bags and picnic coolers. Armed with these devices, professional photographers have bested the worst that nature can present and have brought back from their campaigns photographic trophies of rare beauty.

_____14. Only recently have photographers had to contend with environmental problems.

_____15. Heat is not the only problem photographers have to contend with in the Sahara Desert.

_____16. Photographic equipment should never be taken to places where there are adverse conditions.

_____17. A photographer will brave discomfort and danger to get a great picture.

_____18. The effect of humidity on photographic equipment is usually immediately evident.

_____19. Photographers have not proven to be very creative when it comes to protecting their equipment.

_____20. Sometimes the most basic items provide the best solutions to the problems facing photographers.

EXERCISE 3

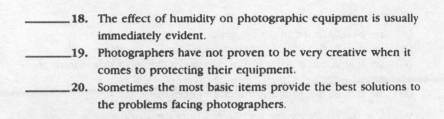

Read the following passages and the inference questions that follow them. Then decide which of the choices, (A), (B), (C), or (D), best answers the question.

QUESTIONS 1–5

Although dinosaurs roamed virtually the whole earth for 160 million years, dinosaur skeletons are relatively scarce. Many dinosaurs are known only from a single tooth or bone chip. The reason is that it takes very special conditions to make a fossil and a lot of luck to find one.

For many years, information about *Tyrannosaurus rex* was sketchy at best. However, in the summer of 1990, the first nearly complete *Tyrannosaurus rex* skeleton ever found was excavated in the Montana badlands. That same year a second, even more complete, skeleton was found in South Dakota. Together these skeletons yielded surprising new insights into the most famous of the dinosaurs, about the anatomy and behavior of *T. rex* and the world in which it lived.

Among the surprising discoveries were that *T. rex* was a far sleeker, but more powerful, carnivore than previously thought, perhaps weighing less than 6½ tons, no more than a bull elephant, and that *T. rex's* habitat was forest, not swamp or plain as previously believed. Moreover, there appears to have been two forms of *T. rex*, the male quite different from the female. Scientists hope that future fossil discoveries and increasingly more sophisticated techniques will provide more accurate and complete information about not only *T. rex* but all the dinosaurs, giving us a window on the world so many millions of years into the past.

1. It can be inferred from the passage that much of what scientists know about *T. rex*
    (A) has been known for many years
    (B) has not come from fossil discoveries
    (C) has been derived from the most sophisticated techniques
    (D) has been recently discovered

2. The passage implies that fossils

   (A) are usually found in the Midwest
   (B) are usually found in beds containing complete skeletons
   (C) are few in comparison to the number of dinosaurs that roamed the earth
   (D) are easy to discover but difficult to excavate

3. Which of the following can be inferred from the passage?

   (A) Interest in fossils is relatively recent.
   (B) It takes advanced techniques to find fossils.
   (C) The search for fossils has been going on for many years.
   (D) Dinosaurs were confined to a relatively small area.

4. Which of the following can be inferred about *T. rex?*

   (A) It was a small but powerful dinosaur.
   (B) It was a strong, meat-eating dinosaur.
   (C) It was a fast, plains-dwelling dinosaur.
   (D) It was a gigantic, forest-dwelling dinosaur.

5. The passage implies which of the following?

   (A) Not all the conclusions scientists make are accurate.
   (B) We have all the information we need about life millions of years ago.
   (C) New discoveries are confirming old theories.
   (D) A whole skeleton is required for information about a dinosaur.

QUESTIONS 6–8

A major revolution for the automated office is electronic mail. The customary postal system requires messages written on paper to be transmitted physically from one location to another. With electronic mail, messages are converted into electronic signals, transmitted anywhere in the world, and then changed back into the original written form, all in several seconds or minutes at most.

Through the use of video screens in company offices, a single document can be transmitted to hundreds of people in dozens of branch offices at the same time. Thus, electronic mail, along with databases, can be an important asset in teleconferences. Furthermore, the use of electronic mail in the form of a "mailbox" attached to a telephone is also of great value. Since in offices many telephone calls go uncompleted on the first attempt, with electronic mail, two-way conversion is not essential, so it reduces telephone use and saves time.

Electronic mail is far more expensive than the postal system, as it must compete for transmission space on satellite, telephone, and cable links. But planned increases in satellite communications should lower the price and assist in the spread of electronic mail.

6. It can be inferred from the passage that the advantages of electronic mail are

   (A) its low cost and efficiency
   (B) its use of the postal system and telephone "mailboxes"
   (C) its role in satellite communications and teleconferencing
   (D) its speed and utility

7. The passage implies that electronic mail

   (A) will be used more often in the future
   (B) will soon outlive its usefulness
   (C) is too costly for most offices
   (D) could never take the place of the current postal system

8. Which of the following can be inferred from the passage?

   (A) Electronic mail saves money but not time.
   (B) Electronic mail has more than one use in the office setting.
   (C) Electronic mail will eventually replace the telephone.
   (D) Electronic mail is not a new phenomenon.

QUESTIONS 9–13

Brown bears are found in Alaska and western Canada. They are first cousins of the grizzly, each belonging to the species *Ursus arctos.* The chief difference in them is size, as brown bears on the average are slightly larger. A full-grown male may weigh 1,500 pounds and stand 9 to 10 feet tall. Like bears everywhere they are creatures of habit that tread the same trails year after year. Brown bears have three gaits: an even, deliberate one that takes them over rough or boggy ground at a steady clip; a quick shuffle; and a fast gallop. They are not only surprisingly fast, but also, for such huge beasts, amazingly agile. They can charge up and climb down nearly vertical inclines. Fishing the streams in summer, they pounce on swift-moving salmon and snatch them with almost simultaneous movements of their paws and mouths. Brown bears are excellent swimmers and love to loll and wallow in the water on warm days. They are also curious and playful. Most manifest a fear of humans, but Alaskans prefer not to test these creatures and usually carry noisemakers of some kind to warn the bears of their presence.

9. It can be inferred from the passage that

   (A) grizzlies are smaller than brown bears
   (B) brown bears do not have the same habits as most bears
   (C) grizzlies are not found in western Canada
   (D) grizzlies and brown bears are not related

10. It is most probable that if a brown bear came across a human in the wild it would

    (A) attack the human
    (B) avoid the human
    (C) not be the least interested in the human
    (D) be friendly toward the human

11. The passage implies that brown bears

    (A) are huge, awkward animals
    (B) can negotiate almost any terrain
    (C) are fierce and bad-tempered
    (D) are not afraid of loud noises

12. The passage suggests that

    (A) it would not be unusual to see a bear cross a deep river
    (B) brown bears catch salmon in quiet pools
    (C) brown bears like to range over new territory
    (D) brown bears are slow but agile

13. Which of the following can be implied from the passage?

    (A) Alaskans have no fear of the brown bear.
    (B) Alaskans do not know very much about the habits of the brown bear.
    (C) Alaskans are not creatures of habit.
    (D) Alaskans have a cautious respect for the brown bear.

QUESTIONS 14–17

Frank Gehry was once considered just another southern California eccentric. It wasn't until the late 1980s that he began receiving international acclaim as one of the world's foremost architects. Outside the mainstream, his random designs have been so unique as to have defied categorization. In the late 1970s he was preoccupied with the notion of things in progress and his belief that buildings are most interesting when still unfinished. To give the impression of a structure in the state of construction, Gehry incorporated exposed studs and joinings, unpainted walls, and transparent skeletal framework in his buildings. In the early 1980s he explored the relation between space, structure, and light.

Like the renderings of artists, Gehry's work is very expressive. His close identity with painters and sculptors has inspired him to infuse his buildings with the qualities of immediacy, spontaneity, and improvisation. His fascination with textures and materials led him to experiment with the effect of combining different building materials, such as plywood, metal, and glass.

While Gehry has achieved international prominence as one of the era's most provocative and creative architects, he continues to experiment with form and structure. With his casual, intuitive approach to design, his buildings continue to demonstrate a high degree of freedom and invention. His work has inspired architects worldwide, who have taken his style and themes to cities around the globe.

14. It is implied in the passage that

    (A) California is known for its conventional artists
    (B) California is internationally known for its architecture
    (C) many Californians are nonconformists
    (D) some people think California is a traditional state

15. The passage suggests that Frank Gehry

    (A) has been labeled a modernist
    (B) had defied definition as a certain type of architect
    (C) has not influenced architects outside the United States
    (D) has always worked within the confines of traditional architectural design

16. From the passage, it can be inferred that Gehry's buildings

    (A) have a very unusual look
    (B) are archaic in form and structure
    (C) fit in well with surrounding structures
    (D) are simplistic and elegant

17. It is most probable that Gehry's designs

    (A) will be limited to certain areas
    (B) will lose their appeal to future architects
    (C) will become conventional over time
    (D) will continue to be evident in urban architecture on a global scale

QUESTIONS 18–21

From a European perspective, the first explorers were engaged in the settlement and discovery of a "new world." However, the history of the United States is but a recent episode in comparison with the history of the North American continent and its people. Between 54 million and 2 million years ago, the continent evolved into the form we know today. At least 15,000 to 20,000 years ago, nomadic hunters began to migrate from Asia across the Bering Strait.

By the fifteenth century, when the European nations were "discovering" America, the country was inhabited by a minimum of 2 million natives. Most of the tribes had developed some kind of agriculture or fishing while remaining as hunters and retaining nomadic characteristics. They roamed the high western plains, hunted mountain valleys, and farmed along the rivers from coast to coast. There was considerable diversity and there were several hundred different languages among the wide-ranging tribes. Several tribes, such as the Iroquois, were very successful in achieving political unity and extending their influence.

The native peoples were well adapted to their environment, and without the aid of the natives, the first European settlers might not have survived. Many native vegetables, such as maize and potatoes, became important staples. Moreover, native trackers guided expeditions and taught hunters and explorers the ways of the land. For years, U.S. history began with Columbus, but today the cultures and contributions of the early inhabitants of the Americas are studied and acknowledged. The story of North America begins with the true origin of the continent and its peoples.

18. The passage implies that

(A) the Europeans were well prepared to live in the "new world"
(B) the Europeans erroneously considered themselves the first settlers in North America
(C) the Europeans were not influenced by the Native Americans
(D) the history of North America begins with its discovery and settlement by the Europeans

19. From the passage it can be inferred that

(A) North America is a relatively new continent
(B) until approximately 20,000 years ago, there were no humans in North America
(C) when the Europeans arrived, North America was uninhabited
(D) Native Americans had as much trouble surviving in North America as the European settlers

20. Which of the following can be inferred from the passage?

(A) Most Native Americans had established permanent settlements by the time the Europeans arrived.
(B) Most Native Americans spoke the same language and had similar customs.
(C) Many Native American tribes had organized societies by the time Europeans arrived.
(D) Once Native Americans began farming, they no longer moved from place to place.

21. The passage suggests that Native Americans

(A) were primitive compared with the European settlers
(B) kept their distance from European settlements
(C) had very little to offer the European settlers
(D) were of benefit to the first settlers

QUESTIONS 22–25

In the twentieth century, people depend on unlimited energy to power their everyday lives. A wide range of energy-run devices and modern conveniences are taken for granted, and although it may seem that we will never be in danger of living without those conveniences, the fact is that many supplies of energy are dwindling rapidly. Scientists are constantly searching for new sources of power to keep modern society running. Whether future populations will continue to enjoy the benefits of abundant energy will depend on the success of this search.

Coal, oil, and natural gas supply modern civilization with most of its power. However, not only are supplies of these fuels limited, but they are a major source of pollution. If the energy demands of the future are to be met without seriously harming the environment, existing alternative energy sources must be improved or further explored and developed. These include nuclear, water, solar, wind, and geothermal power, as well as energy from new, nonpolluting types of fuels. Each of these alternatives, however, has advantages and disadvantages.

Nuclear power plants efficiently produce large amounts of electricity without polluting the atmosphere; however, they are costly to build and maintain, and they pose the daunting problem of what to do with nuclear wastes. Hydroelectric power is inexpensive and environmentally safe, but impractical for communities located far from moving water. Harnessing energy from tides and waves has similar drawbacks. Solar power holds great promise for the future but methods of collecting and concentrating sunlight are as yet inefficient, as are methods of harnessing wind power.

Every source of energy has its disadvantages. One way to minimize them is to use less energy. Conservation efforts coupled with renewable energy resources, such as a combination of solar, water, wind, and geothermal energy and alternative fuels, such as alcohol and hydrogen, will ensure supplies of clean, affordable energy for humanity's future.

22. The passage suggests that

   (A) people use energy without giving great thought to where it's coming from
   (B) the search for energy sources is mainly a problem for the future
   (C) scientists believe we will never have to go without our modern conveniences
   (D) modern society requires a minimum amount of energy to keep it running

23. It can be inferred from the passage that

   (A) most alternative energy sources have proven to be impractical
   (B) many alternative energy sources are environmentally hazardous
   (C) nuclear power solves one problem while creating others
   (D) solar and wind power are not promising for the future

24. From the passage, it can be inferred that to solve our energy problems

   (A) we will have to stop using many of our modern conveniences
   (B) scientists will have to find one major source of nonpolluting energy
   (C) scientists will have to find ways to increase our supplies of coal, oil, and gas
   (D) a combination of conservation and invention will be needed

25. Which of the following can be inferred from the passage?

(A) The search for alternative energy sources is not over.
(B) Our present-energy sources must be eliminated and replaced with alternative sources.
(C) Alternative sources of energy on this planet are very limited.
(D) Demands for energy in the future are likely to decrease.

QUESTIONS 26–28

Manatees and dugongs are members of the mammalian order Sirenia. Completely acquatic, sirenians inhabit the tropical coastal and certain adjacent waters of the West Indies, northern South America, southern North America (Florida), western Africa, and southern Asia to northern Australia. Sirenians live in coastal waters, large rivers, estuaries, lagoons, and connected lakes. Today there exist four species of Sirenia: one dugong and three manatees.

Although similar in appearance to seals and walruses, sirenians are more closely related to elephants. The skin of the sirenian is finely wrinkled and greyish-brown in color. The tail is wide and flat-shaped like a paddle with the exception of the dugong, which has a dolphin-like tail. Sirenians have inspired many a legend about mermaids. The chunky body and homely facial features of a sirenian do not bring to mind the image of a beautiful woman, but the mammal's graceful movements combined with a sailor's faulty vision might give rise to some unusual stories.

26. It is most probable that Sirenians would NOT be found

(A) in the Gulf of Mexico
(B) off the coast of Ghana
(C) in Alaskan waters
(D) on the Brazilian coast

27. It can be inferred from the passage that

(A) some sirenians look like dolphins
(B) physical resemblance among animals does not mean they are related
(C) sirenians look more like elephants than walruses
(D) like seals, sirenians can also live on land

28. The passage suggests that

(A) most sailors were nearsighted
(B) it takes a lot to inspire a legend
(C) legends sometimes have unlikely sources
(D) mermaids were as homely as sirenians

CHAPTER 5

ADDITIONAL READING SKILLS

Introducing Additional Reading Skills
PREREADING QUESTIONS

1. Why do you think people like skiing?

2. What are some popular outdoor sports in your country?

3. What is your favorite sport?

Line Skiing has become a way of life for many people. From the moment the first snowflake falls until the spring thaw, skiers put their skis on their cars and head for the slopes. There are many reasons behind the popularity of this winter sport.

5 Skiing is a true family sport that can be enjoyed by all people, whether 3 or 93 years old. Being able to descend a hill, to turn at will, and enjoy nature at its loveliest are thrills for all age groups.

Skiing is also interesting because it provides a variety of experiences. Snow conditions change hourly as the temperature and weather conditions change during the day. Moreover, every trail is different. Rarely does one pass over the same spot twice.

Improvements in ski equipment, clothing, and ski areas have made the sport more pleasurable, comfortable, and available. Warm, light, down-filled clothing has replaced layers of heavy sweaters. Ski equipment made with modern materials has made skis and poles lighter, more flexible, and suited to people of all ages and abilities. The availability of skiing has also been improved by snow-making equipment. Even in areas of the country that have very little snowfall, snow can be made if the temperature is below 32 degrees.

20 For many people, skiing is an opportunity to enjoy the beauty of the out-of-doors, to challenge their physical abilities, and, finally, to simply have fun. It is a sport enjoyed worldwide and appears to be gaining in popularity constantly.

EXERCISE 1

Answer the following questions.

SKIMMING
Read the passage over quickly.

1. What is the main topic of the passage?

SCANNING
Look over the passage again to find the answers to questions 2-17.

2. Name three things that make skiing fun for all ages.

3. Why do snow conditions change?

4. What kind of clothing do skiers wear today?

5. Why is ski equipment better today?

6. How can people in areas that have little snowfall make skiing available?

In each of the sentences below, underline the detail that is NOT mentioned in the passage.

7. The passage mentions places to ski, ski equipment, ski clothing, and different trails.

8. Compared with the ski clothing of the past, when people wore layers of heavy sweaters, today's ski clothing is warm and light because it is filled with feathers or modern materials.

VOCABULARY QUESTIONS

9. What do you think the word "thaw" in line 2 means?

10. What does the word "trail" in line 10 mean?

INFERENCE

11. What can we infer about the availability of ski areas?

12. In which type of publication would you probably find this passage?

13. What tone does the author take in writing this passage?

    (A) Favorable
    (B) Amused
    (C) Neutral
    (D) Worried

14. The paragraph following this passage probably deals with

    (A) snow-making
    (B) skiing accidents
    (C) the cost of skiing
    (D) ski resorts around the world

15. What is the author's main purpose in the passage?

    (A) To describe
    (B) To persuade
    (C) To inform
    (D) To summarize

16. What conclusions can be drawn from the passage?

17. Which of the following best describes the organization of the passage?

    (A) The author presents the advantages and disadvantages of skiing.
    (B) The author describes skiing.
    (C) The author explains the popularity of skiing and gives reasons.
    (D) The author classifies skiing.

Additional Reading Skills Questions

In the previous chapters of this book, we looked at the main types of questions asked in the Reading Comprehension section of the test, which include main idea, detail, inference, and reference questions. In this chapter, the remaining types of questions that appear in this part of the test will be covered. These are

1. Questions on context

2. Questions on tone and attitude

3. Questions on information that might precede or proceed from the passage

4. Questions on main purpose

5. Questions on drawing conclusions

6. Questions on organization

QUESTIONS ON CONTEXT

There are different types of context questions depending on the particular field of the reading passage.

1. The questions may regard the kind of publication in which the passage may be found.

Examples

> The passage would most likely be found in a textbook on which of the following subjects?

> The passage would most likely be found in . . . .

2. The questions may regard the author of the passage.

Examples

> The passage was most probably written by a specialist in . . . .

> The passage was written most likely by an expert in . . . .

3. The questions may regard the audience for the passage.

Examples

> For whom has the author probably written the passage?

> The audience the author had in mind when writing this passage was most likely a group of . . . .

> The information in this passage would most likely be of interest to . . . .

4. The questions may be about the class for which the passage would be assigned.

Examples

> For what course would the passage probably be assigned?

QUESTIONS ON TONE AND ATTITUDE

These questions ask you about the author's feelings when he or she wrote the passage.

Examples

> The tone of the passage could best be described as . . . .

> What tone does the author take in writing this passage?

In the passage the author may take a strong position for or against something, but passages in this section usually have a neutral tone. The following are examples of strong positive and negative tones.

Examples

The work, a true masterpiece, was written in a day. (positive)

In her brilliant career as an architect, she was renowned not only for the quality of her work but also for the amount of work she produced. (positive)

This system is extravagant of land use and not suitable for many areas of the world. (negative)

These experiments are not only shocking but also a waste of time and money. (negative)

Attitude questions are similar to questions on tone. You must determine the author's opinion or position toward the subject.

Examples

The author's attitude toward . . . could best be described as . . . .

What is the author's attitude toward . . . ?

The author's opinion of . . . could best be described as one of . . . .

How would the author probably feel about . . . ?

Here are some examples of tone or attitude answers:

positive	negative	neutral
humorous	disbelieving	scientific
supportive	depressing	objective
favorable	unfavorable	impersonal

In other attitude questions, you may be asked what you think the author's opinion of four statements would be.

Examples

The author of the passage would most likely agree with which of the following?

Which of the following recommendations would the author most likely support?

QUESTIONS ON INFORMATION COMING BEFORE OR AFTER THE PASSAGE

These questions ask you to suppose the passage is part of a longer work and to guess what the topic of the previous paragraph of the following paragraph would be. In such questions, the beginning of the passage usually gives you a clue as to the previous paragraph, and the end of the passage usually gives you a clue as to the topic that follows.

Examples

The paragraph(s) before this one most probably discussed the . . . .

The paragraph following this one most probably discusses . . . .

What was most probably discussed in the paragraph preceding the passage?

What is most likely the topic of the paragraph following this one?

QUESTIONS ON MAIN PURPOSE

Questions on main purpose ask why the author wrote the passage. These questions appear in place of main idea questions and are the first questions after the passage.

Examples

What is the author's main purpose in the passage?

The author's purpose in writing is to . . . .

Why did the author write the passage?

The answers to these questions begin with infinitives such as

to discuss	to tell how
to mention	to distinguish
to persuade	to illustrate
to summarize	to advise
to compare	to criticize
to describe	to explain

QUESTIONS ON DRAWING CONCLUSIONS

Questions on drawing conclusions are similar to inference questions. These questions ask you to infer from the facts or ideas presented in the passage.

It can be concluded from the passage that . . . .

The passage supports which of the following conclusions?

Which of the following conclusions about . . . is supported by the passage?

Which of the following conclusions about . . . can be drawn from the passage?

QUESTIONS ON ORGANIZATION

Organization questions ask you about the general organization of the passage or of a particular paragraph.

Examples

Which of the following best describes the organization of the passage?

Which of the following statements best describes the organization of the first paragraph?

Here are some examples of the answer to such questions:

Persuasive language is used against . . . .

A general concept is defined, and examples are given.

The author describes . . . .

Several generalizations are presented, from which various conclusions are drawn.

The views of two researchers are described and contrasted.

A specific case is given to describe a general principle.

Sample Reading Passage

Line   Although "lie detectors" are being used by governments, police departments, and businesses that all want guaranteed ways of detecting the truth, the results are not always accurate. Lie detectors are properly called emotion detectors, for their aim is to measure bodily changes that
5   contradict what a person says. The polygraph machine records changes in heart rate, breathing, blood pressure, and the electrical activity of the skin (galvanic skin response, or GSR). In the first part of the polygraph test, you are electronically connected to the machine and asked a few neutral questions ("What is your name?" "Where do you live?"). Your physical
10   reactions serve as the standard (baseline) for evaluating what comes next. Then you are asked a few critical questions among the neutral ones

("When did you rob the bank?"). The assumption is that if you are guilty, your body will reveal the truth, even if you try to deny it. Your heart rate, respiration, and GSR will change abruptly as you respond to the incriminating questions.

15

That is the theory; but psychologists have found that lie detectors are simply not reliable. Since most physical changes are the same across the emotions, machines cannot tell whether you are feeling guilty, angry, nervous, thrilled, or revved up from an exciting day. Innocent people may be tense and nervous about the whole procedure. They may react physiologically to a certain word ("bank") not because they robbed it, but because they recently bounced a check. In either case the machine will record a "lie." The reverse mistake is also common. Some practiced liars can lie without flinching, and others learn to beat the machine by tensing muscles or thinking about an exciting experience during neutral questions.

20

25

QUESTION

1. It can be concluded from the passage that a polygraph test

(A) is the best way to determine a person's guilt
(B) can read a person's thoughts
(C) is the only evidence needed in a court of law
(D) works in principle but not in practice

ANSWER

Answer (A) is not correct because the polygraph is not reliable according to psychologists; therefore, it cannot be the best way to determine a person's guilt. Answer (B) is also incorrect because a polygraph only records physical reactions. Answer (C) is not correct since the passage does not imply that this would be the only evidence needed in a court of law. The best answer is (D), since this is another way of saying that the theory of the polygraph is good but, because it is not reliable, in practice it does not work.

QUESTION

1. What is most likely the subject of the paragraph preceding this passage?

(A) Using lie detectors in the hope that machines will do better to discover the truth
(B) How achievement and aptitude tests measure ability and intelligence
(C) The role of psychologists in fighting crime
(D) An analysis of the criminal mind

ANSWER

Answer (B) is not correct since neither ability nor intelligence has been mentioned in the passage. Answer (C) is also incorrect. Psychologists are not mentioned in the beginning of the passage; they are mentioned later and only to state that they find the machine unreliable, indicating nothing about a role in fighting crime. Answer (D) is incorrect since only one example of the criminal mind is given, at the end of the passage at the mention of those who beat the machine. Therefore, this cannot be the subject that comes before the passage. Answer (A) is the best answer because the beginning of the passage talks about lie detectors and how the machines work to discover the truth.

QUESTION

1. This passage was probably written by a specialist in

    (A) sociology
    (B) anthropology
    (C) mind reading
    (D) criminal psychology

ANSWER

Answer (A) is not correct because a sociologist studies human behavior in groups and does not study the human mind and its related bodily reactions. Answer (B) is also incorrect because an anthropologist studies different human races and their habits and beliefs. Answer (C) is incorrect because a specialist in mind reading will use parapsychology and will not believe in what psychologists have to say. The best answer is (D) since the polygraph supports the opinion of psychologists on the subject of being found guilty or innocent of committing a crime.

QUESTION

1. The author would most probably agree with which of the following statements?

    (A) Polygraphs have no place in our society.
    (B) Physical reactions are not connected to thoughts.
    (C) Machines are no match for psychologists.
    (D) Polygraph tests should not be used as the sole evidence of guilt.

ANSWER

Answer (A) is not correct; although the author does not think that polygraphs are reliable, this statement would be overwhelmingly disapproving and an exaggeration of the author's feelings. Answer (B) is also not correct since the author does not deny this statement, but only indicates how physical reactions may not be reliably determined by the polygraph. Answer (C) is also incorrect.

Machines could be any machines, including computers. This is an exaggerated statement. The best answer is (D) since this statement supports the author's opinion that polygraph tests are unreliable, but it does not exaggerate by ruling out other evidence of guilt.

QUESTION

1. Which of the following statements best describes the organization of the last paragraph?

   (A) Several generalizations are made from which several conclusions are drawn.
   (B) A general concept is defined and examples are given.
   (C) Suggestions for the use of lie detectors are given.
   (D) Persuasive language is used to argue against a popular idea.

ANSWER

Answer (A) is not correct since no generalizations are made. Answer (B) is not correct because no concept is given or defined. Answer (C) is also not correct since suggestions for the use of lie detectors are not given. Answer (D) is the best answer since persuasive language is used to argue against the popular idea of using lie detectors.

QUESTION

1. Why did the author write the passage?

   (A) To illustrate how a lie detector works
   (B) To explain how innocent people are found guilty
   (C) To criticize the use of the lie detector
   (D) To propose ways of using a lie detector

ANSWER

Answer (A) is not correct. The author illustrates how a lie detector works only in the first paragraph, but only in order to make the main point later. Answer (B) is not correct. Although the second paragraph mentions that innocent people might be mistakenly found guilty, the passage is about lie detectors. Answer (D) is also not correct. No mention is made of ways of using a lie detector. Answer (C) is the best answer since the author first describes how a lie detector works and then describes how it is unreliable, and in this way criticizes its use.

Strategies

- Questions on drawing a conclusion are similar to inference questions. To answer these questions, remember to draw a conclusion from the information given in the passage. The answer will not be directly stated in the passage.
- Purpose questions are a combination of inference questions and main idea questions asking you why the author wrote the passage. Again, to answer these questions, draw a conclusion from the whole passage to find the author's purpose in writing it.
- Answers to questions about what probably came before the passage or what will probably come after it are not directly stated in the passage. You must draw a conclusion from the information you find. When answering questions about what was discussed preceding, or before, the passage, look at information in the first sentence or the beginning of the passage. When answering questions about what probably comes after the passage, look at the end of the passage, where there may be an indication or transition as to what will come next.
- When answering tone or attitude questions, remember that tone and attitude are implied in a passage and not stated explicitly. When answering tone questions look for words that are neutral, positive, or negative. Most reading passages in this section of the test are neutral in tone. Beware of answer choices that are strong emotional words. Some questions on attitude refer to passages in which the author takes a position for or against a point. In such cases, beware of answer choices that overstate or exaggerate the author's attitude.

Exercises on Additional Reading Skills

EXERCISE 2

Read the following passages and answer the questions that follow.

QUESTIONS 1-4

Various types of fog are essentially clouds that form at the earth's surface, produced by temperature differences and moisture in the air. As warm, moisture-laden air cools, its relative humidity (the amount of moisture that air can contain, which depends on the temperature) increases. Warm air can hold more water vapor than cold air. So if the air is cooled sufficiently it will reach saturation, or the dew point, at which point the moisture begins to condense out of the air and form water droplets, creating fog.

1. What is the author's main purpose in this passage?

    (A) To describe various types of fog
    (B) To explain how fog is formed
    (C) To define relative humidity
    (D) To compare the effects of warm air and cold air

2. It can be concluded from the passage that

    (A) foggy days are caused by cold nights
    (B) fog is likely to form in desert areas
    (C) hot, humid days are usually followed by cold, foggy nights
    (D) fog could form on a cold evening after a warm day

3. This passage would most likely be written by

    (A) an archaeologist
    (B) a biologist
    (C) a meteorologist
    (D) a psychologist

4. The tone of this passage could best be described as

    (A) humorous
    (B) argumentative
    (C) objective
    (D) persuasive

QUESTIONS 5-9

One theory that integrates diverse findings on hunger, eating, and weight argues that body weight is governed by a set-point, a homeostatic mechanism that keeps people at roughly the weight they are genetically designed to be. Set-point theorists claim that everyone has a genetically programmed basal metabolism rate, the rate at which the body burns calories for energy, and a fixed number of fat cells, which are cells that store fat for energy. These cells may change in size (the amount of fat they contain), but never in number. After weight loss, they just lurk around the body, waiting for the chance to puff up again. According to set-point theory, there is no single area in the brain that keeps track of weight. Rather, an interaction of metabolism, fat cells, and hormones keeps people at the weight their bodies are designed to be. When a heavy person diets, the body slows down to conserve energy (and its fat reserves). When a thin person overeats, the body speeds up to burn energy.

5. The passage would most likely be found in a textbook on which of the following subjects?

   (A) Psychology
   (B) Social studies
   (C) Chemistry
   (D) Biology

6. What is most likely the topic of the paragraph following this one?

   (A) A different theory on body weight
   (B) The importance of a proper diet
   (C) The relation between activity and weight
   (D) How to keep fat cells from enlarging

7. It can be concluded from the passage that

   (A) a genetically thin person can easily gain weight
   (B) it is impossible for genetically predisposed overweight people to lose weight
   (C) people don't have as much control over their body weight as they might think
   (D) humans are genetically designed to be overweight

8. The author's attitude toward the subject of weight could best be described as

   (A) emotional
   (B) disbelieving
   (C) depressing
   (D) scientific

9. The writer's purpose in writing this passage is to

   (A) inform
   (B) illustrate
   (C) criticize
   (D) compare

QUESTIONS 10-14

Traditionally, mental tests have been divided into two types. Achievement tests are designed to measure acquired skills and knowledge, particularly those that have been explicitly taught. The proficiency exams required by some states for high school graduation are achievement tests. Aptitude tests are designed to measure a person's ability to acquire new skills or knowledge. For example, vocational aptitude tests can help you decide whether you would do better as a mechanic or musician. However, all mental tests are in some sense achievement tests because they assume some sort of past learning or experience with certain objects, words, or situations. The difference between achievement and aptitude tests is one of degree and intended use.

10. The author's main purpose in this passage is to

    (A) show the importance of testing
    (B) relate a story about aptitude and achievement tests
    (C) compare and contrast achievement and aptitude tests
    (D) criticize the use of testing to measure a person's ability

11. This passage would most likely appear in

    (A) an art journal
    (B) a novel
    (C) a psychology book
    (D) a medical journal

12. Which of the following conclusions can be drawn from this passage?

    (A) Aptitude and achievement tests are interchangeable.
    (B) An aptitude test might be helpful to a person contemplating a career move.
    (C) All high school students should take proficiency exams.
    (D) Tests are a means of acquiring skills and knowledge.

13. The paragraph preceding this one most likely deals with

    (A) other types of psychological testing
    (B) the relation between education and achievement
    (C) career choices
    (D) the requirements for high school graduation

14. The author's attitude toward the subject of testing is

    (A) indifferent
    (B) critical
    (C) objective
    (D) emotional

QUESTIONS 15-19

In 1983 a new type of phonograph disc reached the marketplace, which showed promise of eventually taking over the recording industry. It was called the compact disc and made use of two technical systems: digital recording and laser beams. All recording until the advent of the compact disc was analog recording, which recorded the vibrations of sound waves on a track. With analog recording, there was always a bit of slippage, which added distortion. Digital recording is a completely different process, one in which the distortion is so small that it can be said to be effectively eliminated. Thus the fidelity of the compact disc is extremely high.

Because the indentations on the compact disc pass under a laser beam, no solid device is in contact with the disc, and therefore there is no friction, and wear is eliminated. With a minimum of care, the compact disc should last indefinitely. This is in contrast to the relatively short life of an analog recording.

Another advantage of the compact disc is the system of identifying numbers that allows for random access to any song on the recording with the push of a button.

Because of the improved qualities and advantages of the compact disc, production has increased significantly since its introduction. Although analog recording continues, it is expected to be relegated to a nostalgic past as the CD becomes the recording format of the future.

15. Why did the author write this passage?
    (A) To present the advantages of the compact disc
    (B) To compare recent improvements in recording
    (C) To criticize analog recording
    (D) To support the idea of change in the music industry

16. The tone of the passage could best be described as
    (A) positive
    (B) negative
    (C) humorous
    (D) argumentative

17. The paragraph that precedes this passage most likely deals with
    (A) the other uses of laser beams
    (B) nostalgia in the 1990s
    (C) major stars in the recording industry
    (D) recording methods before 1983

18. This passage would probably be part of assigned reading in which of the following courses?
    (A) Architectural design
    (B) Electrical engineering
    (C) Music history
    (D) Marketing and management

19. According to the passage, it can be concluded that
    (A) people will eventually stop buying compact discs because they last indefinitely
    (B) people didn't enjoy good music until the advent of the compact disc
    (C) analog records will eventually be difficult to obtain
    (D) compact discs require a lot of special care

QUESTIONS 20-24

John Muir was born in Dunbar, Scotland, in 1838, but grew up in Wisconsin. He walked from the Ohio River a thousand miles to the Gulf of Mexico, where he planned to continue south to explore the jungles of the Amazon. However a bout of malaria turned his sights west to California, where he arrived in 1868, immediately falling in love with the land.

Over the next decade Muir became well known as a Sierra Nevada mountaineer, explorer, and naturalist. Later Muir built another more significant career upon his first. He became the nation's foremost conservationist. Yosemite National Park was established in 1890 essentially because of Muir's recommendations.

Two years later he helped found the Sierra Club, which originally limited its conservation activities to "preserving the forests and other natural features of the Sierra Nevada Mountains" before it branched out in recent years to tackle global issues.

In 1903 Muir lured Theodore Roosevelt away from his presidential entourage to spend three nights in Yosemite. Later the President remarked to his party that the time he spent talking conservation with Muir was "the greatest day of my life!" His administration was to make the most sweeping conservation effort in the nation's history.

20. In this passage the author's purpose is to

    (A) defend John Muir's conservation efforts
    (B) describe how the Sierra Club was formed and then expanded
    (C) distinguish between John Muir and Theodore Roosevelt
    (D) relate biographical information about John Muir

21. In what type of textbook would this passage probably appear?

    (A) Botany
    (B) American history
    (C) Anthropology
    (D) Economics

22. Which of the following best describes the organization of the passage?

    (A) The author compares Muir's views on conservation with Theodore Roosevelt's.
    (B) The author defines the concept of conservation and gives examples.
    (C) The author describes the life and times of John Muir.
    (D) The author defends the efforts of John Muir.

23. The author's opinion of John Muir could best be described as

    (A) critical
    (B) respectful
    (C) pessimistic
    (D) humorous

24. Which of the following could be concluded from the passage?

(A) John Muir influenced conservation legislation in the Roosevelt administration.
(B) Founding the Sierra Club was John Muir's chief objective in life.
(C) John Muir probably would have made a good president.
(D) Roosevelt preferred the city to the country.

QUESTIONS 25-30

During the 1920s, African-American culture as embodied in music, art, and literature flourished as never before. In their works, poets, dramatists, and novelists sought to define their culture and engender pride in racial heritage. The outpouring of African-American literature during the 1920s almost came to a standstill during the Great Depression of the 1930s but reemerged with explosive force in the 1940s with Richard Wright's *Native Son*, Chester Himes's *Lovely Crusade*, and Ann Petry's *The Street*, among other novels, as well as the plays and poetry of Langston Hughes. In the 1950s important developments in drama took place with a generation of black playwrights, including Alice Childress, Ted Shine, William Branch, and Lorraine Hansberry, who wrote the prizewinning drama *A Raisin in the Sun*.

The 1960s gave rise to the Black Arts movement. Drama and fiction flourished, often written in the rhythm and language of black working classes. The 1970s and 1980s continued that tradition but also saw the works of black women poets, essayists, dramatists, and fiction writers take the spotlight, making a significant contribution to literature by exploring the themes of black women's experiences. Fiction writers Toni Morrison and Alice Walker, both Pulitzer Prize winners, are two of the finest American writers of this century. Other notable black women writers of other genres, impressive in talent and number, have come into their own, making their voices heard within a literary tradition from which they were excluded for many generations and making African-American literature richer than ever before.

25. The author of this passage would most likely be

(A) a politician
(B) a member of the clergy
(C) an educator
(D) a scientist

26. The author's attitude toward African-American women writers is

(A) disappointed
(B) supportive
(C) neutral
(D) negative

27. The author's main purpose in writing this passage is to

    (A) present a history of African-American literature
    (B) argue the importance of the Black Arts movement
    (C) emphasize the achievements of African-American artists
    (D) explain the difference between male and female African-American authors

28. The paragraph preceding this passage would most likely be about

    (A) early African-American culture
    (B) life during the Great Depression
    (C) the Black Arts movement of the 1960s
    (D) the future of African-American literature

29. Which of the following conclusions could be drawn from this passage?

    (A) There were no black playwrights before the 1950s.
    (B) The Great Depression was a period that fostered creativity.
    (C) The sixties were not good years for African-American writers.
    (D) Women have added a new dimension to African-American literature.

30. Which of the following statements best describes the organization of the first paragraph?

    (A) Various types of African-American culture are compared and contrasted.
    (B) Historical facts about African-American culture are presented.
    (C) Persuasive opinions on African-American literature are given.
    (D) A story about African Americans is narrated.

QUESTIONS 31-35

One step beyond automated machines is the industrial robot, the heart and brain of which is the microcomputer. Unlike most automated machines, industrial robots can be programmed to do a variety of tasks that are usually accomplished by human factory workers. Like their human counterparts, industrial robots can be switched from one job to another and can be programmed to handle new tasks. Thus far, robots have found their greatest use in assembling mechanical components. However, they are swiftly branching from basic assembly operations to construction and mining, and their most glamorous use of all, the exploration of oceans and outer space.

31. The author's main purpose in writing this passage is to

    (A) describe the industrial robot and its uses
    (B) narrate a story about the industrial robot
    (C) compare the industrial robot to human factory workers
    (D) argue the advantages of the industrial robot

32. The author's reaction to an innovative form of transportation, such as the electric car, would most likely be

    (A) positive
    (B) negative
    (C) confusion
    (D) surprise

33. The paragraph following this passage would most likely be about

    (A) types and uses of automated machines
    (B) how industrial robots are used in exploration
    (C) the uses of the microcomputer
    (D) how robots assemble mechanical components

34. This passage would most likely be found in

    (A) an entertainment magazine
    (B) a medical journal
    (C) a book of short stories
    (D) a popular science journal

35. It can be concluded from this passage that

    (A) robots will never replace human factory workers
    (B) industrial robots are not as versatile as automated machines
    (C) the microcomputer will soon be used in automated machines
    (D) additional uses will be found for the industrial robot

QUESTIONS 36–40

Probably the most important factor governing the severity of forest fires is weather. Hot, dry weather lowers the moisture content of fuels. Once a fire has started, wind is extremely critical because it influences the oxygen supply and the rate of spread. Forest type and forest conditions are also important factors. For example, fire is more likely to occur in conifers than in hardwoods; slash-covered or brushy areas are especially hazardous because the rate at which combustion consumes fuel is proportional to fuel volume and surface area.

Some fires are caused by lightning; others are caused by people. Those caused by people may be accidental or intentional (incendiary). The causes of fire in the United States show large regional differences. In the Rocky Mountains more than 70 percent of the fires are caused by lightning, whereas incendiary fires amount to only about 1 percent. In contrast, more than 40 percent of the fires in the South are incendiary, whereas lightning causes only 1 percent.

36. In this passage the author's main purpose is to

    (A) argue
    (B) inform
    (C) persuade
    (D) entertain

37. Which of the following best describes the organization of the passage?

   (A) A comparison and contrast of the factors governing forest fires is followed by a list of causes.
   (B) A description of the conditions affecting forest fires is followed by a description of the causes.
   (C) An analysis of factors related to forest fires is followed by an argument against the causes of fires.
   (D) Several generalizations about forest fires are followed by a series of conclusions.

38. It can be concluded from this passage that

   (A) there are not many people living in the Rocky Mountain area
   (B) there are more fires in hardwood forests than in pine forests
   (C) winter is the worst season for fires
   (D) fire prevention techniques vary from region to region

39. The paragraph following this passage would most likely be about

   (A) the causes of hot, dry weather
   (B) the various uses of hardwoods
   (C) methods of controlling fires
   (D) the geographical differences between the Rocky Mountain area and the Southern states

40. The author of this passage would most likely be

   (A) a forest ranger
   (B) a meteorologist
   (C) a historian
   (D) a business person

QUESTIONS 41–44

Scientists disagree about the place of instinct in human behavior. Sociobiologists argue that even complicated forms of human behavior can have an instinctive basis. They believe we have an inborn urge to propagate our own genes and those of our biological relatives. Social customs that enhance the odds of such transmission survive in the form of kinship bonds, courtship rituals, altruism, taboos against female adultery, and many aspects of social life. Other social scientists have argued that human behavior can be explained solely by learning. Psychologists today generally take a middle path. They acknowledge that human behavior is influenced by our biological heritage, but most doubt that either imprinting or true instincts occur in human beings.

41. The author's attitude toward the subject of human behavior is

    (A) condescending
    (B) humorous
    (C) negative
    (D) neutral

42. It can be concluded from the passage that

    (A) social scientists agree on a single theory of human behavior
    (B) today's psychologists are not interested in exploring human behavior
    (C) human behavior is influenced by a variety of factors
    (D) the desire to procreate is learned behavior

43. This passage would most likely be required reading in which of the following courses?

    (A) Biology
    (B) Geography
    (C) Psychology
    (D) Philosophy

44. The paragraph preceding this passage is most likely about

    (A) imprinting
    (B) courtship rituals
    (C) taboos
    (D) instincts

QUESTIONS 45-50

In 1912 Frederick G. Hopkins and Casimir Funk suggested that specific human diseases, such as beriberi, rickets, and scurvy, were caused by the absence of certain nutritional substances in the diet. These were termed vitamines ("vital amines"), because the first such substance isolated, thiamin (vitamin B1), was an amine (a compound containing an amino group). When other such essential substances were isolated and analyzed, they proved not to be amines, but the term vitamin was retained to refer to any essential growth factor required in very small amounts. Many vitamins have been discovered since that time. Although the functions of some vitamins are unknown, many have been shown to be coenzymes.

Letters of the alphabet were first used to describe the mysterious nutritional factors. These letters (A, B, C, D, E, K, and others) have persisted. It was found, however, that some factors actually consisted of more than one substance. The original B factor has been shown to consist of more than a dozen entities. These factors are now designated as specific substances, for example, thiamin (B1), riboflavin (B2), pantothenic acid (B3), and three related substances, and niacin. Because these commonly occur together, they are referred to as the B-complex vitamins.

45. The information in this passage would most likely be of interest to a student of

    (A) engineering
    (B) nutrition
    (C) psychology
    (D) farming

46. Which of the following best describes the author's tone?

    (A) Argumentative
    (B) Negative
    (C) Curious
    (D) Neutral

47. This passage would most likely appear in which chapter of a science book?

    (A) Plants and Their Benefits
    (B) The Transfer of Energy
    (C) Food and Human Needs
    (D) Human Diseases

48. The author's main purpose in this passage is to

    (A) compare and contrast nutritional substances
    (B) define vitamins and relate their history
    (C) identify the vitamins humans need
    (D) argue in favor of taking vitamins

49. It can be concluded from this passage that

    (A) vitamins cannot be used to treat disease
    (B) vitamins work separately in the body
    (C) most vitamins are not essential to good health
    (D) scientists still don't know everything about vitamins

50. Which of the following statements best describes the organization of the passage?

    (A) A general concept is defined, and examples are given.
    (B) Persuasive language is used to argue against a popular idea.
    (C) Suggestions for the use of vitamins are given.
    (D) Several generalizations are made from which several conclusions are drawn.

PART TWO

Reading Comprehension Practice Tests

Read the following passage.

Some researchers distinguish primary emotions, which are thought to be universal, from secondary emotions, which include variations and blends that are specific to cultures. The primary emotions are usually identified with fear, anger, sadness, joy, surprise, and disgust. Other psychologists doubt that surprise and disgust are true emotions; they also think that this list omits universal emotions, such as love, hope, empathy, and pride, that are difficult to measure physiologically.

Example I

1. What is the main idea of the passage?
   (A) Some emotions are difficult to measure.
   (B) All emotions are universal.
   (C) A distinction is made between primary and secondary emotions.
   (D) All emotions are primary.

The main idea of the passage is that some researchers make a distinction between primary and secondary emotions. Therefore, you should choose answer (C).

Example II

1. According to the passage, other psychologists think that the emotions of surprise and disgust are

   (A) true emotions
   (B) difficult to measure
   (C) not true emotions
   (D) secondary emotions

The passage states that "other psychologists doubt that surprise and disgust are true emotions." Therefore, you should choose answer (C).

QUESTIONS 1-11

Line   Supernovas are the most powerful and spectacular outbursts known in nature. What is called a Type II supernova is due to the collapse of a massive star, at least eight times as massive as the sun, that has used up its main nuclear fuel and produced a nickel-iron core. When this core can no
5   longer support the pressure of the star's outer layers, it collapses to form a neutron star of immense density. Over 2,500 million tons of neutron star material could be packed into a matchbox. Its temperature is around 100,000 million degrees centigrade. Multitudes of neutrons are produced in the collapsed star, which pass directly through the star into space, and
10   this release of neutrons causes the core to respond with a shock wave that moves outward. When it meets the material that is falling inward, the result is a catastrophic explosion. Sometimes most of the star's material is blown away, leaving only a small, incredibly dense remnant that may be a neutron star or, in extreme cases, a black hole.
15   A supernova is often more than 500 million times as luminous as the sun. A supernova remnant (SNR) may be detectable as a pulsar, an example of which is the Crab Nebula, known to be a remnant of the supernova observed in the year 1054. The 1987 supernova in the Large Cloud of Magellan had a low peak luminosity by supernova standards, only
20   about 250 million times that of the sun. At its brightest the supernova shone as a star between magnitudes 2 and 3, even though it was 170,000 light-years away.

1. What is the main topic of the passage?

   (A) The heat of supernovas
   (B) The formation and power of a supernova
   (C) The role of shock waves in a supernova
   (D) The density of a neutron star

2. The word "it" in line 11 refers to the

   (A) shock wave
   (B) neutron star
   (C) core of the collapsed star
   (D) catastrophic explosion

3. According to the passage, which of the following is NOT true about the 1987 supernova?

   (A) It was located in the Large Cloud of Magellan.
   (B) It was 170,000 light-years away.
   (C) It shone as a star between magnitudes 3 and 4.
   (D) It had a low peak luminosity.

4. In line 16 the word "detectable" is closest in meaning to

   (A) assumed
   (B) known
   (C) perceptible
   (D) audible

5. Which of the following words can best be substituted for "remnant" in line 17?

   (A) Characteristic
   (B) Relic
   (C) Specter
   (D) Remainder

6. The author of this passage is most likely

   (A) a botanist
   (B) an economist
   (C) a mathematician
   (D) an astronomer

7. The word "Multitudes" in line 8 is closest in meaning to

   (A) magnitudes
   (B) groups
   (C) many
   (D) temperatures

8. The word "catastrophic" in line 12 is closest in meaning to

   (A) violent
   (B) colorful
   (C) scientific
   (D) luminous

9. What can be inferred from the passage about supernovas?

   (A) They only happen to pulsars.
   (B) The sun is a remnant of a supernova.
   (C) They occur when two stars collide.
   (D) They sometimes result in a black hole.

10. According to the passage, what marks the beginning of a supernova?

    (A) A star has grown too big.
    (B) A star is born.
    (C) The neutrons of a star become very dense.
    (D) A massive star uses up its main nuclear fuel.

11. Where in the passage does the author state what is left of a star after a supernova occurs?

    (A) Line 5
    (B) Line 8
    (C) Line 12
    (D) Line 20

QUESTIONS 12-23

Line Horace Pippin, as an African-American soldier during World War I, was
wounded in his right arm. He discovered, however, that by keeping his
right wrist steady with his left hand, he could paint and draw. Pippin was
not trained, but his artistic sensitivity and intuitive feel for two-
5   dimensional design and the arrangement of color and patterns made him
one of the finest primitive artists America has produced.

   Pippin did a series of paintings on the abolitionist John Brown and
one of his war experiences, but he shied away from social issues for the
most part and achieved his greatest success with scenes of the people and
10   places of his hometown of West Chester, Pennsylvania. His Domino
Players, featuring four women gathered around a wooden table in a simple
kitchen setting, is an excellent example of his rural domestic scenes.

12. According to the passage, which of the following is NOT true about primitive art?

    (A) It is two-dimensional.
    (B) Colors and patterns are important.
    (C) Artists do not have to be trained for it.
    (D) It is used primarily for painting portraits.

13. Horace Pippin discovered he could paint and draw

    (A) during World War I
    (B) when he completed his artistic training
    (C) when someone reminded him of his artistic sensitivity
    (D) by holding his right wrist steady with his left hand

14. Where in the passage is the name of Pippin's hometown mentioned?

    (A) Line 6
    (B) Line 10
    (C) Line 4
    (D) Line 9

15. It may be inferred from the passage that Pippin

    (A) had a simple upbringing
    (B) was obsessed with the subject of abolition
    (C) was devastated by his war experiences
    (D) wanted nothing to do with his past

16. The word "arrangement" in line 5 could best be replaced by which of the following?

    (A) Purpose
    (B) Fixture
    (C) Composition
    (D) Blend

17. With which of the following statements would the author probably agree?

    (A) Horace Pippin was a poorly trained, mediocre artist.
    (B) Primitive art is an excuse for lack of training and talent.
    (C) Horace Pippin made a significant contribution to American art.
    (D) Horace Pippin placed too much emphasis on social issues in his work.

18. This passage would most likely be required reading in which course?

    (A) Anthropology
    (B) Drama
    (C) Sociology
    (D) Art history

19. The word "intuitive" in line 4 is closest in meaning to

    (A) educated
    (B) artistic
    (C) intense
    (D) instinctive

20. The phrase "shied away from" in line 8 is closest in meaning to

    (A) postponed
    (B) avoided
    (C) painted
    (D) feared

21. The word "gathered" in line 11 can best be replaced by

    (A) seated
    (B) scattered
    (C) collected
    (D) domesticated

22. The word "rural" in line 12 is closest in meaning to

    (A) primitive
    (B) urban
    (C) country
    (D) beautiful

23. The author includes the fact that Pippin was wounded

    (A) because violence was a major theme in his paintings
    (B) as an example of a rural domestic scene
    (C) to show that he succeeded in spite of a handicap
    (D) in order to classify him as a primitive artist

QUESTIONS 24–33

Line   In the folklore of the Navajo people, it was said that frogs and toads fell from the sky when it rained. The phenomenon that gave rise to this belief involved the spadefoot toad, which remains dormant beneath the Sonoran Desert of Arizona, avoiding the heat and drought for as long as eight or
5   nine months. With the onset of summer thunderstorms, however, the toads respond to the vibrations of drumming raindrops and emerge, as if fallen from the sky with the rain, to begin their brief and frantic mating season.

        The male spadefoot sits in a muddy pool and fills the night with his
10   calls, attempting to attract a female of the same species. Once a female joins him, she may lay as many as 1,000 eggs in the small pool of life-sustaining rainwater. From that point it's a race against the elements for the young, who must hatch and mature with remarkable speed before the pool evaporates beneath the searing desert sun. As the pool grows
15   smaller and smaller, it becomes thick with tadpoles fighting for survival in the mud, threatened not only by the loss of their watery nest but also by devouring insects and animals. In as few as nine days after fertilization of the eggs, those lucky enough to survive develop through each tadpole stage and finally emerge as fully formed toads. After gorging themselves on
20   insects, the young toads, like their parents, burrow underground, where they will lie dormant awaiting the next summer's storms.

24. What does the passage mainly discuss?

    (A) Navajo folklore
    (B) Weather in the Sonoran Desert of Arizona
    (C) The habits of the spadefoot toad
    (D) The mating rituals of the male spadefoot

25. According to the passage, the spadefoot toad

    (A) is dormant for as long as nine months
    (B) reproduces during winter rains
    (C) eats leaves and grasses
    (D) develops very slowly

26. Which of the following is NOT true of the spadefoot?

    (A) They are active only three to four months a year.
    (B) The female lays her eggs in pools of water.
    (C) The searing desert sun is their only enemy.
    (D) Many tadpoles die before they reach maturity.

27. It can be concluded from the passage that

    (A) spadefoot toads could exist for years without rain
    (B) the Navajo legends are based on acute observations
    (C) spadefoot toads are well adapted to their environment
    (D) the chances of a tadpole's becoming an adult are very great

28. The author is most likely a

    (A) botanist
    (B) biologist
    (C) chemist
    (D) geographer

29. This passage is most likely followed by a passage on

    (A) weather patterns in the Sonoran Desert
    (B) methods of reproduction among insects
    (C) dwellings of the Navajo people
    (D) other desert animals

30. The word "frantic" in line 7 is closest in meaning to

    (A) lengthy
    (B) excited
    (C) froglike
    (D) dangerous

31. The word "elements" in line 12 could best be replaced by

    (A) weather
    (B) time
    (C) environment
    (D) thunderstorms

32. The word "gorging" in line 19 is closest in meaning to

    (A) mating
    (B) digging
    (C) enjoying
    (D) devouring

33. Where in the passage is the geographic location that the spadefoot toads inhabit mentioned?

    (A) Line 1
    (B) Line 9
    (C) Line 3-4
    (D) Line 16-17

QUESTIONS 34-41

Line   Contrary to the frantic pace of today's economic environment, the origin
        of banking and capital markets in the United States was not an overnight
        phenomenon. The form of organization called a corporation developed
        very slowly in the states. Early joint-stock companies, in which each
5   member was responsible for the obligations of the mutual enterprise, were
        principally nonprofit corporations for religious worship, philanthropy,
        education, or land companies. Commercial corporations didn't make their
        appearance until the early to mid-1700s, with a Connecticut trading
        corporation, a Massachusetts wharf company, a number of fire insurance
10   and water supply companies, and the United Company of Philadelphia,
        which was organized to promote industry. By the late 1700s, particularly
        the period from 1783 to 1789, the corporate structure expanded when
        numerous corporations were organized for building roads, canals, and
        bridges and for banking.
15   America's first private commercial bank, the Bank of North America,
        was chartered by Congress on December 31, 1781. The Bank of New York
        and the Bank of Massachusetts followed in 1784, but all these banks were
        local and limited. In December 1791, national banking originated with the
        first national bank, which opened its main office in Philadelphia. In 1816,
20   the second national bank was chartered for twenty years. Meanwhile state
        banks began to proliferate throughout the country.
            The late 1800s saw an emergence of investment banking houses that
        promoted mergers in railroads, utilities, and factories and provided the
        capital for expansion. Commercial banking also flourished, but after a high
25   rate of bank failures, the Federal Reserve System was established in 1913

to correct deficiencies in existing banking legislation on the national and state levels. The Federal Reserve Act set the foundation for modern banking.

34. Where in the passage does the author define joint-stock companies?

 (A) Lines 4-7
 (B) Lines 10-12
 (C) Lines 13-16
 (D) Lines 20-24

35. Which of the following is NOT true about the origin of banking in the United States?

 (A) The first private commercial bank was chartered by Congress in 1781.
 (B) The early banks were limited in scope.
 (C) Banking developed rapidly in the United States.
 (D) The first national bank was located in Philadelphia.

36. According to the passage, when did commercial corporations appear in the United States?

 (A) After 1800
 (B) Before the 1600s
 (C) Around 1750
 (D) In 1791

37. What does the passage mainly discuss?

 (A) How mergers provided the capital for expansion of railroads, utilities, and factories
 (B) The establishment of the Federal Reserve System
 (C) How commercial corporations developed from nonprofit companies
 (D) The origin and development of banks and corporations

38. The words "all these banks" in line 17 refer to

 (A) private commercial banks
 (B) national banks
 (C) investment banking houses
 (D) nonprofit corporations

39. Where in the passage does the author's focus move from corporations to banks?

 (A) Lines 7-8
 (B) Line 15
 (C) Line 20
 (D) Line 25

40. Which of the following could be used to replace the word "phenomenon" in line 3?

    (A) Factor
    (B) Occurrence
    (C) Development
    (D) Examination

41. In line 24, the word "capital" is closest in meaning to

    (A) building materials
    (B) large city
    (C) financial resources
    (D) corporate structure

QUESTIONS 42-50

Line   The invention of the electric telegraph gave birth to the communications industry. Although Samuel B. Morse succeeded in making the invention useful in 1837, it was not until 1843 that the first telegraph line of consequence was constructed. By 1860 more than 50,000 miles of lines
5   connected people east of the Rockies. The following year, San Francisco was added to the network.
         The national telegraph network fortified the ties between East and West and contributed to the rapid expansion of the railroads by providing an efficient means to monitor schedules and routes. Furthermore, the
10   extension of the telegraph, combined with the invention of the steam-driven rotary printing press by Richard M. Hoe in 1846, revolutionized the world of journalism. Where the business of news gathering had been dependent upon the mail and on hand-operated presses, the telegraph expanded the amount of information a newspaper
15   could supply and allowed for more timely reporting. The establishment of the Associated Press as a central wire service in 1846 marked the advent of a new era in journalism.

42. The main topic of the passage is

    (A) the history of journalism
    (B) the origin of the national telegraph
    (C) how the telegraph network contributed to the expansion of railroads
    (D) the contributions and development of the telegraph network

43. According to the passage, how did the telegraph enhance the business of news gathering?

    (A) By adding San Francisco to the network
    (B) By allowing for more timely reporting
    (C) By expanding the railroads
    (D) By monitoring schedules and routes for the railroads

44. The author's main purpose in this passage is to

    (A) compare the invention of the telegraph with the invention of the
         steam-driven rotary press
    (B) propose new ways to develop the communications industry
    (C) show how the electric telegraph affected the communications industry
    (D) criticize Samuel B. Morse

45. The word "Rockies" in line 5 refers to

    (A) a telegraph company
    (B) the West Coast
    (C) a mountain range
    (D) a railroad company

46. It can be inferred from the passage that

    (A) Samuel Morse did not make a significant contribution to the
         communications industry
    (B) Morse's invention did not immediately achieve its full potential
    (C) The extension of the telegraph was more important than its
         invention
    (D) Journalists have the Associated Press to thank for the birth of the
         communications industry

47. The word "revolutionized" in line 12 is closest in meaning to

    (A) destroyed
    (B) revolved
    (C) gathered
    (D) transformed

48. According to the passage, which of the following is NOT true about the
    growth of the communications industry?

    (A) Morse invented the telegraph in 1837.
    (B) People could use the telegraph in San Francisco in 1861.
    (C) The telegraph lead to the invention of the rotary printing press.
    (D) The telegraph helped connect the entire nation.

49. The word "gathering" in line 13 refers to

    (A) people
    (B) information
    (C) objects
    (D) substances

50. This passage would most likely be found in a

    (A) U.S. history book
    (B) book on trains
    (C) science textbook
    (D) computer magazine

PRACTICE 2 TEST

Read the following passage.

Some researchers distinguish primary emotions, which are thought to be universal, from secondary emotions, which include variations and blends that are specific to cultures. The primary emotions are usually identified with fear, anger, sadness, joy, surprise, and disgust. Other psychologists doubt that surprise and disgust are true emotions; they also think that this list omits universal emotions, such as love, hope, empathy, and pride, that are difficult to measure physiologically.

Example I

1. What is the main idea of the passage?

   (A) Some emotions are difficult to measure.
   (B) All emotions are universal.
   (C) A distinction is made between primary and secondary emotions.
   (D) All emotions are primary.

The main idea of the passage is that some researchers make a distinction between primary and secondary emotions. Therefore, you should choose answer (C).

Example II

1. According to the passage, other psychologists think that the emotions of surprise and disgust are

   (A) true emotions
   (B) difficult to measure
   (C) not true emotions
   (D) secondary emotions

The passage states that "other psychologists doubt that surprise and disgust are true emotions." Therefore, you should choose answer (C).

QUESTIONS 1-11

Line   Today's cars are smaller, safer, cleaner, and more economical than their predecessors, but the car of the future will be far more pollution-free than those on the road today. Several new types of automobile engines have already been developed that run on alternative sources of power, such as
5   electricity, compressed natural gas, methanol, steam, hydrogen, and propane. Electricity, however, is the only zero-emission option presently available.

        Although electric vehicles will not be truly practical until a powerful, compact battery or other dependable source of current is available,
10   transportation experts foresee a new assortment of electric vehicles entering everyday life: shorter-range commuter electric cars, three-wheeled neighborhood cars, electric delivery vans, bikes, and trolleys.

        As automakers work to develop practical electrical vehicles, urban planners and utility engineers are focusing on infrastructure systems to
15   support and make the best use of the new cars. Public charging facilities will need to be as common as today's gas stations. Public parking spots on the street or in commercial lots will need to be equipped with devices that allow drivers to charge their batteries while they shop, dine, or attend a concert. To encourage the use of electric vehicles, the most convenient
20   parking in transportation centers might be reserved for electric cars.

        Planners foresee electric shuttle buses, trains, buses, and neighborhood vehicles all meeting at transit centers that would have facilities for charging and renting. Commuters will be able to rent a variety of electric cars to suit their needs: light trucks, one-person three-wheelers, small cars,
25   or electric/gasoline hybrid cars for longer trips, which will no doubt take place on automated freeways capable of handling five times the number of vehicles that can be carried by a freeway today.

1. The following electrical vehicles are all mentioned in passage EXCEPT

   (A) vans
   (B) trains
   (C) planes
   (D) trolleys

2. The author's purpose in the passage is to

(A) criticize conventional vehicles
(B) support the invention of electric cars
(C) narrate a story about alternative energy vehicles
(D) describe the possibilities for transportation in the future

3. The passage would most likely be followed by details about

(A) automated freeways
(B) pollution restrictions in the future
(C) the neighborhood of the future
(D) electric shuttle buses

4. The word "compact" in line 9 is closest in meaning to

(A) long-range
(B) inexpensive
(C) concentrated
(D) square

5. In the second paragraph the author implies that

(A) a dependable source of electric energy will eventually be developed
(B) everyday life will stay much the same in the future
(C) a single electric vehicle will eventually replace several modes of transportation
(D) electric vehicles are not practical for the future

6. According to the passage, public parking lots of the future will be

(A) more convenient than they are today
(B) equipped with charging devices
(C) much larger than they are today
(D) as common as today's gas stations

7. This passage would most likely be found in a

(A) medical journal
(B) history book
(C) popular psychology periodical
(D) textbook on urban planning

8. The word "charging" in this passage refers to

(A) electricity
(B) credit cards
(C) aggression
(D) lightening

9. The word "foresee" in line 21 could best be replaced with

   (A) count on
   (B) invent
   (C) imagine
   (D) rely on

10. The word "Commuters" in line 23 refers to

   (A) daily travelers
   (B) visitors
   (C) cab drivers
   (D) shoppers

11. The word "hybrid" in line 25 is closest in meaning to

   (A) combination
   (B) hazardous
   (C) futuristic
   (D) automated

QUESTIONS 12-23

Line   Red Rock Canyon, part of the Red Rock Recreation Lands in Nevada, is an
escarpment of crimson Aztec sandstone cliffs and canyon walls that reveal
the geologic history of the area. Bands of sediment layers tell of a deep-sea
bed that 400 million years ago rose eastward to a shoreline in present-day
5   western Utah. As the ancient sea grew progressively more shallow, about
225 million years ago, marine limestone and shales were overlaid by
sediments washed in from emerging land areas. As the water in the
shallow inland seas evaporated, salts and minerals were deposited in thick
beds and fluctuating shorelines created intermixed beds of limestone,
10   shales, and minerals. Sediments from this period gave the canyon its name.
Their red color was created from the weathering of iron compounds
within. About 180 million years ago the area became arid and was covered
in sand dunes more than 2,000 feet deep, which became cemented into
the Aztec sandstone that is prominent in the canyon today. Its alternating
15   hues of red, yellow, and white are believed to have resulted from
groundwater percolating through the sand and leaching out the oxidized
iron.
          The most significant geologic feature of the area is the Keystone
Thrust Fault, a fracture in the earth's crust. Sixty-five million years ago,
20   intense pressure thrust one rock plate over another, a phenomenon that
can clearly be seen in the contrasting bands of gray limestone and red
sandstone, where the gray limestone cap is actually older than the
sandstone beneath it. The Keystone is one of the most easily identifiable
thrust faults to be found anywhere.

12. With what topic is the passage mainly concerned?

   (A) The creation of the Keystone Thrust Fault
   (B) How Red Rock Canyon acquired its name
   (C) The formation of Aztec sandstone
   (D) The geologic history of Red Rock Canyon

13. The author of this passage is most likely

   (A) an animal rights activist
   (B) a geologist
   (C) a public relations writer
   (D) a public works engineer

14. The word "progressively" in line 5 is closest in meaning to

   (A) suddenly
   (B) mysteriously
   (C) naturally
   (D) gradually

15. In line 19, the word "phenomenon" refers to

   (A) contrasting bands of limestone and sandstone
   (B) one rock plate thrust over another
   (C) a fracture in the earth's crust
   (D) a significant geologic feature

16. Which of the following can be concluded from this passage?

   (A) Red Rock Canyon was created in a relatively short time span.
   (B) The location of a rock layer is not always an indication of its age.
   (C) The expansion of the sea bed played a significant role in the creation of Red Rock Canyon.
   (D) Emerging land areas eventually caused the sea to evaporate.

17. In line 22, the word "identifiable" could best be replaced by which of the following?

   (A) Observable
   (B) Significant
   (C) Discovered
   (D) Created

18. According to the passage, the red of the canyon walls is primarily a result of

   (A) groundwater percolating through the sand
   (B) the weathering of iron compounds
   (C) the evaporation of the inland sea
   (D) intense pressure on rock plates

19. The word "fluctuating" in line 9 is closest in meaning to

    (A) intermixing
    (B) flooding
    (C) changing
    (D) withdrawing

20. The word "arid" in line 12 is closest in meaning to

    (A) dead
    (B) uninhabited
    (C) reddened
    (D) dry

21. The word "its" in line 14 refers to

    (A) Aztec sandstone
    (B) Shorelines
    (C) Cement
    (D) Hues

22. According to the passage, when did Red Rock Canyon become dry?

    (A) 400 million years ago
    (B) 225 million years ago
    (C) 180 million years ago
    (D) 65 million years ago

23. According to the passage, all of the following remained after the sea evaporated EXCEPT

    (A) shale
    (B) sandstone
    (C) limestone
    (D) minerals

QUESTIONS 24–33

Line Sylvia Earle, a marine botanist and one of the foremost deep-sea explorers, has spent over 6,000 hours, more than seven months, underwater. From her earliest years, Earle had an affinity for marine life, and she took her first plunge into the open sea as a teenager. In the years since then she has
5 taken part in a number of landmark underwater projects, from exploratory expeditions around the world to her celebrated "Jim dive" in 1978, which was the deepest solo dive ever made without cable connecting the diver to a support vessel at the surface of the sea.

Clothed in a Jim suit, a futuristic suit of plastic and metal armor,
10 which was secured to a manned submarine, Sylvia Earle plunged vertically into the Pacific Ocean, at times at the speed of 100 fee per minute. On

reaching the ocean floor, she was released from the submarine and from that point her only connection to the sub was an 18-foot tether. For the next 2½ hours, Earle roamed the seabed taking notes, collecting
15   specimens, and planting a U.S. flag. Consumed by a desire to descend deeper still, in 1981 she became involved in the design and manufacture of deep-sea submersibles, one of which took her to a depth of 3,000 feet. This did not end Sylvia Earle's accomplishments.

24.   When did Sylvia Earle discover her love of the sea?

   (A)   In childhood
   (B)   During her 6,000 hours underwater
   (C)   After she made her deepest solo dive
   (D)   Well into her adulthood

25.   It can be inferred from the passage that Sylvia Earle

   (A)   is not interested in the scientific aspects of marine research
   (B)   is uncomfortable in tight spaces
   (C)   does not have technical expertise
   (D)   has devoted her life to ocean exploration

26.   The author's opinion of Sylvia Earle is

   (A)   critical
   (B)   supportive
   (C)   ambivalent
   (D)   disrespectful

27.   According to the passage, the Jim suit was made of

   (A)   extra tough fabric
   (B)   rubber and plastic
   (C)   plastic and metal
   (D)   chain mail

28.   The word "consumed" in line 15 means

   (A)   devoured
   (B)   defeated
   (C)   exhausted
   (D)   overwhelmed

29.   What will the paragraph following this passage probably be about?

   (A)   Sylvia Earle's childhood
   (B)   More information on the Jim suit
   (C)   Earle's achievements after 1981
   (D)   How deep-sea submersibles are manufactured

30. The main purpose of this passage is

    (A) to explore the botany of the ocean floor
    (B) to present a short biography of Sylvia Earle
    (C) to provide an introduction to oceanography
    (D) to show the historical importance of the Jim dive

31. Which of the following is NOT true about the Jim dive?

    (A) It took place in 1981
    (B) Sylvia Earle took notes while on the ocean floor
    (C) It was performed in the Pacific Ocean
    (D) The submarine that Sylvia Earle was connected to was manned

32. The word "affinity" in line 3 is closest in meaning to

    (A) fear
    (B) indifference
    (C) fondness
    (D) dislike

33. Where in the passage does the author mention how long Sylvia Earle
    spent on the ocean floor?

    (A) Line 2
    (B) Line 6
    (C) Line 11
    (D) Line 14

QUESTIONS 34–41

Line   Most of the early houses built in America were suited to farm life, as it was
        not until cities became manufacturing centers that colonists could survive
        without farming as their major occupation. Among the earliest farmhouses
        in America were those built in Plymouth Colony. Generally they consisted
5   of one large rectangular room on the ground floor, called a hall or great
        room and having a fireplace built into one of the walls, and a loft
        overhead. Sometimes a lean-to was attached alongside the house to store
        objects such as spinning wheels, firewood, barrels, and tubs. The
        furnishings in the great room were sparse and crudely built. Tabletops and
10   chest boards were split or roughly sawed and often smoothed only on one
        side. Benches took the place of chairs, and the table usually had a trestle
        base so it could be dismantled when extra space was required. One or two
        beds and a six-board chest were located in one corner of the room. The
        fireplace was used for heat and light, and a bench often placed nearby for
15   children and elders, in the area called an inglenook.

The original houses in Plymouth Colony were erected within a tall fence for fortification. However, by 1630 Plymouth Colony had 250 inhabitants, most living outside the enclosure. By 1640 settlements had been built some distance from the original site. Villages began to emerge
20 throughout Massachusetts and farmhouses were less crudely built. Windows brought light into homes and the furnishings and decor were more sophisticated.

As more diversified groups of immigrants settled the country, a greater variety of farmhouses appeared, from Swedish log-style houses in
25 the Delaware Valley to saltbox houses in Connecticut, Dutch-Flemish stone farmhouses in New York, and clapboard farmhouses in Pennsylvania. From Georgian characteristics to Greek revival elements, farmhouses of varied architectural styles and building functions populated the landscape of the new frontier.

34. The main idea of the passage is

(A) life in Plymouth Colony
(B) the history of the American farmhouse
(C) how to build an American farmhouse
(D) where immigrants settled in America

35. Which of the following is NOT mentioned as part of the furnishings in a farmhouse?

(A) Rocking chair
(B) Six-board chest
(C) Bench
(D) Trestle-based table

36. According to the passage, the earliest farmhouses were built in

(A) Delaware Valley
(B) Massachusetts
(C) Pennsylvania
(D) Connecticut

37. In line 12, the word "it" refers to a

(A) trestle base
(B) chest board
(C) space
(D) table

38. It can be inferred from the passage that

(A) sophisticated tools were available to the early immigrants
(B) the major occupation in Plymouth Colony was carpentry
(C) the extended family lived together in the farmhouse
(D) cloth was imported from England

39. The passage was most probably written by a specialist in American

   (A) urban planning
   (B) architecture
   (C) immigration
   (D) farming

40. The word "emerge" in line 19 could best be replaced with

   (A) proceed
   (B) come out
   (C) settle
   (D) appear

41. According to the passage, all of the following are true EXCEPT

   (A) Immigrants brought a greater variety to the design of houses.
   (B) The inglenook was a bench for children and elders.
   (C) Most early colonists were farmers.
   (D) Early farmhouses consisted of a large room and a loft.

QUESTIONS 42-50

Line   Four West Indian geckos, with human assistance, have recently entered
       the United States. The yellow-headed gecko, the ashy gecko, the reef
       gecko, and the ocellated gecko are presently inhabiting the tropical areas
       of the Keys and the tip of southern Florida. The Mediterranean gecko also
5   arrived along the Gulf coast some time ago, via the West Indies. The only
       other geckos in the United States live in the Southwest. In extreme
       southern California, the leaf-fingered gecko lives in dry, rocky country and
       scampers over boulders at night, hiding by day in crevices. The banded
       gecko inhabits the desert areas from southern California to southern
10   Texas. This three- to four-inch nocturnal gecko has a slender, tapered tail
       and stalks insects by raising itself high on its legs, cocking its head, and
       twitching its tail nervously before leaping on its prey. In courtship, the tail
       is also waved by the male as he approaches the female.
             Although most lizards are excellent climbers, the geckos are able to
15   walk on smooth surfaces with the help of unique clinging devices under
       the toes. Also, the undersides of most geckos have pads of large scales,
       each of which bear microscopic hairs with hundreds of branches having
       minute, blunt ends that press against the surface that the gecko is on,
       enabling the gecko to cling to almost any surface. Like other lizards,
20   geckos have the ability to shed their tails if attacked by an enemy. The
       stump heals and a new tail is grown in approximately the same shape as
       the original. Unlike most lizards, most geckos have no moveable eyelids.
       The nocturnal geckos have vertical pupils, which contract in bright light.
       All geckos, except several New Zealand species, lay eggs. The eggs have a
25   tough, white shell and are laid under stones, behind window shutters, or
       under bark.

42. The author's main purpose is to

    (A) compare lizards and geckos
    (B) describe the behavior and environment of geckos
    (C) analyze the life of a gecko
    (D) illustrate the habits of geckos

43. The habitat of the leaf-fingered gecko is described in lines

    (A) 1–4
    (B) 6–8
    (C) 8–10
    (D) 16–18

44. It can be concluded from the passage that

    (A) lizards are better climbers than geckos
    (B) lizards and geckos have very little in common
    (C) geckos are herbivores
    (D) geckos can live in both humid and dry climates

45. In line 1, the author uses the words "human assistance" to mean

    (A) people brought West Indian geckos to these areas
    (B) West Indian geckos were raised by humans
    (C) humans saved West Indian geckos from extinction
    (D) West Indian geckos reached these places while escaping from humans

46. What is the most likely subject of the paragraph following this passage?

    (A) The story of the journeys of West Indian geckos
    (B) Information on how baby geckos hatch and develop
    (C) A description of geckos native to North America
    (D) A history of the southern California desert

47. According to the passage, the banded gecko

    (A) lives in dry, rocky country
    (B) has a short, stout tail
    (C) recently entered the United States
    (D) is nocturnal

48. Which of the following is closest in meaning to the word "nocturnal" in line 10?

    (A) Quick-moving
    (B) Very poisonous
    (C) Cold-blooded
    (D) Active at night

49. The word "minute" in line 18 is closest in meaning to

    (A) very quick
    (B) very small
    (C) extremely hard
    (D) extremely fast

50. The passage would be of most interest to

    (A) statisticians
    (B) history professors
    (C) biology students
    (D) social scientists

PRACTICE **3** TEST

Directions

In this section you will read several passages. Each passage is followed by several questions. For each question choose the one best answer from (A), (B), (C), and (D). Then on your answer sheet fill in the space that corresponds to the letter you have chosen. Your answers should be based on what is stated or implied in the passage.

Read the following passage.

Some researchers distinguish primary emotions, which are thought to be universal, from secondary emotions, which include variations and blends that are specific to cultures. The primary emotions are usually identified with fear, anger, sadness, joy, surprise, and disgust. Other psychologists doubt that surprise and disgust are true emotions; they also think that this list omits universal emotions, such as love, hope, empathy, and pride, that are difficult to measure physiologically.

Example I

1. What is the main idea of the passage?
   (A) Some emotions are difficult to measure.
   (B) All emotions are universal.
   (C) A distinction is made between primary and secondary emotions.
   (D) All emotions are primary.

The main idea of the passage is that some researchers make a distinction between primary and secondary emotions. Therefore, you should choose answer (C).

Example II

1. According to the passage, other psychologists think that the emotions of surprise and disgust are

   (A) true emotions
   (B) difficult to measure
   (C) not true emotions
   (D) secondary emotions

The passage states that "other psychologists doubt that surprise and disgust are true emotions." Therefore, you should choose answer (C).

QUESTIONS 1-11

Line   Research has indicated that dyslexia has biological origins, and most
investigators now suspect that dyslexic children read poorly as a result of
a highly specific language problem, sometimes called "phonological
unawareness." Dyslexic children cannot easily learn to read because they
5   have trouble associating printed letters with the sounds of speech. A
similar problem occurs in congenitally deaf people who have mastered the
linguistic complexities and subtleties of sign language but have trouble
learning to read.

   Evidence also exists suggesting that the root cause for much dyslexia
10   is a problem with processing very rapidly changing sensory stimuli. For
example, studies have shown that dyslexic children have trouble making
accurate distinctions between similar auditory signals. They often cannot
hear the difference between speech sounds such as "pah," "dah," and
"bah." Recently, differences have been noted between the visual
15   pathways of dyslexics and those of nondyslexics that suggest a comparable
problem with fast-changing visual stimuli. Researchers have also found
several other neuroanatomical abnormalities in the temporal lobe and in
other areas of the brain. All of these studies are extremely valuable in
helping researchers understand the mechanisms underlying reading
20   problems so that dyslexic children can be accurately identified and more
efficiently helped.

1. What is the main purpose of the passage?

   (A) To change current ideas about dyslexia
   (B) To explore the causes of dyslexia
   (C) To distinguish between dyslexia and congenital deafness
   (D) To cite examples of dyslexic behavior

2. According to the passage, "phonological unawareness" means

   (A) trouble with hearing and sensory stimuli
   (B) inability to distinguish between auditory signals
   (C) problems associating printed letters and sounds
   (D) abnormalities in the temporal lobe

3. At what point in the passage does the author state where neuroanatomical abnormalities are located?

   (A) Line 10
   (B) Line 12
   (C) Lines 17-18
   (D) Lines 20-21

4. The author compares the problems of dyslexic children with

   (A) dyslexic adults
   (B) the subtleties of sign language
   (C) the visual pathways of other dyslexics
   (D) the problems of congenitally deaf people

5. This passage would be of most interest to

   (A) children
   (B) writers
   (C) educators
   (D) scientists

6. The words "congenitally deaf" in line 6 refer to people who are

   (A) partially deaf
   (B) capable of learning
   (C) deaf and dyslexic
   (D) deaf since birth

7. The word "stimuli" in line 10 is closest in meaning to

   (A) input
   (B) problems
   (C) research
   (D) association

8. As used in line 12, the word "They" refers to

   (A) researchers
   (B) deaf people
   (C) dyslexics
   (D) nondyslexics

9. The words "temporal lobe" in line 17 refer to

   (A) the ear lobe
   (B) an area of research
   (C) a part of the brain
   (D) a kind of dyslexia

10. Both dyslexic people and deaf people have a problem with

    (A) hearing

    (B) speaking

    (C) reading

    (D) writing

11. Which of the following can be inferred from the passage?

    (A) "Pah" and "dah" are easily distinguished by deaf children.

    (B) Deaf people are more intelligent than dyslexics.

    (C) Nondyslexics contribute nothing to dyslexia research.

    (D) Research in the field of deafness may be helpful in the study of dyslexia.

QUESTIONS 12–23

Line Barn owls, of the family Tytonidae, are anatomically different enough from other owls to merit their own family in the order Strigiformes. Instead of the more or less rounded face of most owls, the barn owl has a heart-shaped face and lacks the usual tufted earlike feathers. The common

5 barn owl is from 12 to 18 inches long and has a white face, cinnamon buff back, buff or white breast, and relatively small eyes. The legs are fairly long, feathered to the toes, and, like those of all owls, very strong and equipped with sharp, powerful, curved claws, the outer ones being reversible, although they are usually directed backward.

10   Barn owls nest in hollow trees, caves, and buildings on every continent except Antarctica and have adapted so well to living near humans that in some areas they seem to have forsaken natural nesting places in favor of man-made ones. They hunt in open spaces and have the largest range of any nocturnal bird. They use their eyesight to locate prey,

15 but their hearing is so highly developed that they can hunt small mammals in total darkness. Barn owls are economically valuable because of their preference for small, crop-destroying mammals.

12. It can be inferred from the passage that owls hunt for food in

    (A) forests

    (B) swampy areas

    (C) fields

    (D) caves

13. According to the passage, barn owls have a highly developed sense of

    (A) taste

    (B) sight

    (C) hearing

    (D) touch

14. All of the following are features of the barn owl EXCEPT

   (A) small eyes
   (B) curved claws
   (C) white face
   (D) black breast

15. Which of the following is NOT a customary nesting place for barn owls?

   (A) Trees
   (B) Fields
   (C) Caves
   (D) Buildings

16. This passage is mainly concerned with

   (A) Economic benefits of the barn owl
   (B) Where the barn owl got its name
   (C) Physical description and behavior of barn owls
   (D) Why there are no barn owls in Antarctica

17. The word "merit" in line 2 could best be replaced by

   (A) adapt to
   (B) grow into
   (C) be different from
   (D) be entitled to

18. The word "those" in line 7 refers to

   (A) toes
   (B) owls
   (C) claws
   (D) legs

19. The word "fairly" in line 6 is closest in meaning to

   (A) barely
   (B) somewhat
   (C) extremely
   (D) nicely

20. The word "they" in line 12 refers to

   (A) natural nesting places
   (B) barn owls
   (C) humans
   (D) open spaces

21. In line 12, the word "forsaken" could best be replaced by

   (A) abandoned
   (B) substituted
   (C) chosen
   (D) preferred

22. The words "economically valuable" as used in line 16 mean that the
    barn owl

    (A) is a national treasure
    (B) is worth a lot of money
    (C) prevents farmers from losing money on crop losses
    (D) saves farmers money by eating bad crops

23. This passage would most likely be found in

    (A) a book on agriculture
    (B) a photographer's handbook
    (C) a United States atlas
    (D) an encyclopedia of animal life

QUESTIONS 24-33

Line   *Laser* is an acronym for *light amplification by stimulated emission of
       radiation.* Stimulated emission is a variation of spontaneous emission, a
       process that occurs in atoms when an electron in a ground, or unexcited
       state, is knocked into a higher state when energy is applied to the system.
5   As the electron drops back into ground state, a photon, or particle of light,
       is released. As de-excitation occurs in millions of atoms, photons are
       released in a random fashion, and light is emitted in every direction.
       Stimulated emission, however, causes an increase in the number of
       photons traveling in a particular direction. An optical cavity, the space
10   formed by two reflective surfaces facing each other, is used to control the
       direction of the beam. There are solid-state, gas, and liquid lasers, and by
       subjecting lasing materials to various types of energy—electrical,
       magnetic, or sonic—scientists have been able to control the laser output
       to suit various functions and applications.
15   In industry, the laser has proven to be a very versatile tool,
       particularly for cutting and welding. Lasers are now also used in
       high-speed printing and in the creation of three-dimensional images, called
       holograms. Laser tracking and ranging systems have been developed, using
       light signals to measure distance rather than the radio signals of radar. The
20   use of the laser in biological and medical applications is also rapidly
       expanding, and the laser is already being used with great success in certain
       surgical procedures. In the field of communications the laser, used in
       conjunction with fiber-optic networks, is capable of carrying much more
       information than conventional wires and is setting the stage for the
       "electronic superhighway" of the near future.

24. Where in the passage does the author define optical cavity?

    (A) Lines 3-4
    (B) Lines 9-11
    (C) Lines 16-18
    (D) Lines 22-23

25. The main topic of the second paragraph is
    (A) the applications of the laser
    (B) fiber-optic networks
    (C) measuring distances with lasers
    (D) the uses of lasers in medicine

26. The author's main purpose in this passage is to
    (A) persuade
    (B) entertain
    (C) illustrate
    (D) inform

27. It can inferred from the passage that lasers are rapidly becoming
    (A) obsolete in today's world
    (B) more limited in scope
    (C) a vital part of modern society
    (D) less flexible in their uses

28. According to the passage, scientists have been able to control laser output by
    (A) controlling the direction of the beam
    (B) subjecting lasing materials to various types of energy
    (C) increasing the number of photons traveling in a particular direction
    (D) using a variety of lasing materials

29. What happens when an electron drops back into ground state?
    (A) A particle of light is released.
    (B) Excitation occurs.
    (C) Energy is applied to the system.
    (D) There is an increase in the number of photons traveling in one direction.

30. In line 23, the words "in conjunction with" could best be replaced with which of the following phrases?
    (A) At a crossroads
    (B) Aside from
    (C) In combination with
    (D) In addition to

31. The author mentions all of the following types of lasers EXCEPT
    (A) solid-state
    (B) sonic
    (C) gas
    (D) liquid

32. The word "versatile" in line 15 is closest in meaning to
    (A) flexible
    (B) stimulating
    (C) energetic
    (D) worthless

33. According to the passage, the "electronic superhighway"
    (A) will replace the laser
    (B) has nothing to do with lasers
    (C) will utilize lasers
    (D) will be in competition with lasers

QUESTIONS 34-41

Line   A new class of 75-foot yachts has replaced the 12-meter racing vessels that
       populated the America's Cup races since the late 1800s, but the
       excitement and challenge of the race remain unabated. Only once in the
       history of the America's Cup has the prize left the shores of the United
5   States. That coup was perpetrated by Australian businessman Alan Bond
       and his yacht Australia II, skippered by John Bertrand in 1983.
            Dating back to the middle of the nineteenth century, the America's
       Cup is the oldest international sporting trophy of any kind. In 1851, at the
       invitation of England's Earl of Wilton, Commodore of the Royal Yacht
10   Squadron, the New York Yacht Club sent the schooner America across the
       Atlantic to race against the British. The sole American entry went against
       seventeen of Britain's racing yachts and finished ahead of the Aurora by 18
       minutes. The prize, an ornate silver urn, named "The Hundred Guinea
       Cup" for its cost, was handed over to the winners and was known
15   thereafter as the "America's Cup."
            Six years after the race, the Cup was given to the New York Yacht
       Club with the understanding that any foreign yacht club could challenge
       for it. Despite twenty-five challenges, the Cup remained in America's
       hands until 1983. However, the only man to have lost the cup in 132 years,
20   Dennis Connor, was not one to accept defeat. During a grueling four and
       a half months of elimination races in some of the most testing conditions
       in which 12-meter boats had ever sailed, Dennis Connor won the right to
       compete for the Cup. In September 1988 Connor's controversial 60-foot
       catamaran, Stars and Stripes, sailed past Michael Fay's equally controversial
25   130-foot yacht, New Zealand, to win back the prize in a court-challenged
       victory. The final court decision kept the cup on American soil but led to
       the demise of the complicated formula that dogged the 12-meter yachts for
       so many years.

34. With which of the following statements would the author agree?

    (A) The America's Cup races should be relegated to an event of the past.
    (B) The British are responsible for America's winning streak.
    (C) The America's Cup is an important and stimulating event.
    (D) There should be a return to the old formula for America's Cup racing boats.

35. The passage preceding this one is most likely about

    (A) other international yacht races
    (B) how to sail in foul weather
    (C) boating terms
    (D) the construction of sailing vessels

36. The main idea of this passage is

    (A) how to win the America's Cup
    (B) why Australia won the America's Cup
    (C) the role of the British in the America's Cup
    (D) the history of the America's Cup

37. Which of the following conclusions about the America's Cup is supported by the passage?

    (A) The America's Cup race is losing its popularity.
    (B) The Australians will not be contenders in the future.
    (C) The America's Cup will never again leave the shores of the United States.
    (D) The next America's Cup race will not be as controversial as the last.

38. The words "that coup" in line 5 refer to

    (A) the Australian win
    (B) Alan Bond
    (C) the yacht Australia II
    (D) the America's Cup race

39. According to the passage, how many times was the Cup challenged before the Americans lost it?

    (A) 18
    (B) 25
    (C) 60
    (D) 132

40. The word "unabated" in line 3 means

    (A) undiminished
    (B) unopposed
    (C) controversial
    (D) significant

41. The word "testing" in line 21 could best be replaced by

(A) frightening
(B) wondrous
(C) challenging
(D) analytical

QUESTIONS 42-50

Line   In January 1964, President Lyndon B. Johnson called for a war on poverty
in his State of the Union Address. Eight months later the Economic
Opportunity Act and other legislation were enacted. Almost 100 million
dollars was authorized for ten programs to be conducted by the Office of
5   Economic Opportunity, including Job Corps, Volunteers in Service to
America (VISTA), work training and work-study programs, and aids for
small businesses.

Not only was President Johnson dedicated to fighting poverty, but he
vowed to end racial discrimination as well, bringing about the passage of
10   the Civil Rights Law of 1964. The Urban Mass Transportation Act of 1964
and the Wilderness Preservation Act were also passed that year.

With those achievements and a landslide victory in the 1964
presidential election to bolster his resolve, President Johnson in his 1965
State of the Union Address called for a vast program to achieve the "Great
15   Society," including a massive program to end crippling diseases, a
doubling of the war on poverty, enforcement of the Civil Rights Law,
elimination of barriers to the right to vote, reform of immigration laws, an
education program of scholarships and loans, and a massive effort to
establish more recreational and open space.

20   At the president's urging, the first session of the 89th Congress
passed the most significant amount of legislation since the New Deal. The
new legislation included large-scale programs to aid schools, the
establishment of the Medicare program to provide medical care for the
elderly, another voting rights act, two housing acts to help low-income
25   families obtain housing, reform of immigration laws, and the establishment
of the National Foundation on the Arts and Humanities.

42. The main topic of this passage is

(A) President Johnson's State of the Union addresses
(B) Lyndon Johnson's fight against poverty
(C) The legislation enacted by the 89th Congress
(D) The accomplishments of the Johnson administration

43. It can be inferred from the passage that Lyndon Johnson was

(A) supported by wealthy industrialists
(B) not a conservationist
(C) dedicated to improving life through social programs
(D) a believer in less government spending and more business growth

44. Which of the following is NOT mentioned as legislation passed during the first session of the 89th Congress?

    (A) Job Corps
    (B) Medicare
    (C) Housing acts
    (D) School aid

45. What is the author's attitude toward Lyndon Johnson?

    (A) Disregard
    (B) Suspicion
    (C) Admiration
    (D) Indifference

46. The word "bolster" in line 13 means to

    (A) dissipate
    (B) strengthen
    (C) declare
    (D) weaken

47. According to the passage, when was the Wilderness Preservation Act passed?

    (A) 1965
    (B) During the 89th Congress
    (C) During the New Deal
    (D) 1964

48. Where in the passage does the author state how much money was authorized for the Office of Economic Opportunity programs?

    (A) Lines 3-4
    (B) Line 10
    (C) Line 17
    (D) Line 22

49. The word "landslide" in line 12 is closest in meaning to

    (A) an avalanche
    (B) the legislation
    (C) a majority of votes
    (D) a close election

50. The word "discrimination" in line 9 is closest in meaning to

    (A) impoverishment
    (B) tolerance
    (C) differentiation
    (D) prejudice

Read the following passage.

Some researchers distinguish primary emotions, which are thought to be universal, from secondary emotions, which include variations and blends that are specific to cultures. The primary emotions are usually identified with fear, anger, sadness, joy, surprise, and disgust. Other psychologists doubt that surprise and disgust are true emotions; they also think that this list omits universal emotions, such as love, hope, empathy, and pride, that are difficult to measure physiologically.

Example I

1. What is the main idea of the passage?

   (A) Some emotions are difficult to measure.
   (B) All emotions are universal.
   (C) A distinction is made between primary and secondary emotions.
   (D) All emotions are primary.

The main idea of the passage is that some researchers make a distinction between primary and secondary emotions. Therefore, you should choose answer (C).

Example II

1. According to the passage, other psychologists think that the emotions of surprise and disgust are

    (A) true emotions
    (B) difficult to measure
    (C) not true emotions
    (D) secondary emotions

The passage states that "other psychologists doubt that surprise and disgust are true emotions." Therefore, you should choose answer (C).

QUESTIONS 1-11

Line   Ragtime, developed primarily by black pianists, is a style of composed piano music that was popular from the 1890s to about 1915. It is a style of jazz characterized by an elaborately syncopated rhythm in the melody and a steadily accented accompaniment. Ragtime quickly gained popularity
5   after its first appearances, reaching millions on a national scale through sheet music, player pianos, ragtime songs, and arrangements for dance and marching bands. The leading ragtime composer was Scott Joplin, known as the "Kind of Ragtime," whose most famous piano piece, "Maple Leaf Rag," was published in 1899.
10   Ragtime piano music has a generally standard form, duple meter (2/4, or two beats per measure) performed at a moderate march tempo. The pianist's right hand plays a highly syncopated melody, while the left hand steadily maintains the beat with an "oom-pah" accompaniment. A ragtime piece usually consists of several similar melodies that take such
15   forms as AA BB A CC DD or Introduction AA BB CC DD EE, where each letter represents a melodic phrase. "Maple Leaf Rag: is a classic example of ragtime. About three minutes long, it has the standard AA BB A CC DD form, and each section is 16 bars in length. The opening melody, in march tempo, features the typical ragtime right-hand syncopations.
20   The forms of ragtime derive from European marches and dances, but the rhythms are rooted in African-American folk music, the same rich body of music that became a vital source of jazz. Early jazz musicians often used ragtime melodies as introductions to their improvisations. With its syncopations, steady beat, and piano style, ragtime played an integral part in the jazz legacy.

1. The author's main purpose in the passage is to

    (A) compare ragtime and jazz
    (B) criticize the compositions of Scott Joplin
    (C) show how ragtime is arranged
    (D) discuss the origin and elements of ragtime

2. Ragtime reached people nationwide through all of the following EXCEPT

   (A) compositions for orchestras
   (B) player pianos
   (C) sheet music
   (D) arrangements for marching bands

3. According to the passage, the letters A in AA and B in BB each represent

   (A) march tempo
   (B) oom-pah accompaniment
   (C) a melodic phrase
   (D) syncopated melody

4. Which of the following is NOT characteristic of ragtime?

   (A) Fast march tempo
   (B) Sixteen-bar sections
   (C) Left-hand accompaniment
   (D) Highly syncopated melody

5. This passage would be part of required reading in which of the following courses?

   (A) African-American history
   (B) Music appreciation
   (C) Art history
   (D) Social studies

6. The word "rooted" as used in line 21 means

   (A) attached to the ground
   (B) unmoving
   (C) derived from
   (D) never changing

7. The word "it" in line 17 refers to

   (A) melodic phrase
   (B) each letter
   (C) ragtime
   (D) "Maple Leaf Rag"

8. Which of the following conclusions can be made from this passage?

   (A) Ragtime music is complex and hard to identify.
   (B) Ragtime was popular only with African Americans.
   (C) Ragtime has an easily recognizable rhythm.
   (D) Ragtime is a completely different form of music than jazz.

9. The word "elaborately" in line 3 is closest in meaning to

(A) eloquently
(B) simply
(C) intricately
(D) melodically

10. In line 13, the word "maintains" may best be replaced by

(A) withholds
(B) keeps
(C) exaggerates
(D) interrupts

11. The word "improvisations" in line 23 is closest in meaning to

(A) compositions
(B) dances
(C) marches
(D) legacies

QUESTIONS 12-23

Line   In North America there are two forms of bison, the plains bison and the
        woodland bison. The plains bison once ranged from Pennsylvania and
        Georgia to the Rockies, north to the edge of the Canadian forest, and south
        onto the central plateau of Mexico. The bison has a great tolerance to
5   cold. When blizzards rage across the North American prairie, bison lower
        their heads and face directly into the storm. In winter the vegetation on
        which these animals feed may be hidden beneath a deep blanket of snow;
        however, this does not present a problem, for the bison use their hooves
        and massive heads to clear away the snow and then feed on the grasses
10   below. Bison are strong survivors and have few predators except for
        humans, who reduced their population to the point at which, around
        1900, there were fewer than a thousand plains bison left. However, with
        protection and careful breeding they have been brought back to the point
        where their numbers can be multiplied at will. Large herds presently range
15   on both government and private lands where they are protected. Other
        endangered species need the same planning and protection.

12. The author's main purpose in the passage is

(A) to spread awareness that the bison is near extinction
(B) to show the differences between the plains bison and woodland
    bison
(C) to explain how the bison finds food after heavy snowfall
(D) to provide an example of an endangered species avoiding extinc-
    tion

13. In line 14, the word "their" refers to

    (A) numbers
    (B) predators
    (C) humans
    (D) plains bison

14. The passage supports which of the following conclusions?

    (A) Bison will eventually be extinct.
    (B) Bison are more fragile than they appear.
    (C) The bison population can be controlled.
    (D) Bison were native to a limited territory.

15. The topic of the passage following this one would likely be about

    (A) the endangered grizzly of North America
    (B) the diversity of climates in America
    (C) national parks of North America
    (D) cold-blooded animals of the Southwestern desert

16. According to the passage, where would bison be found during a severe winter storm?

    (A) Seeking shelter behind boulders
    (B) In the open
    (C) In caves
    (D) Behind trees

17. The word "range" as used in line 14 mean to

    (A) surround
    (B) move about
    (C) cook on a stove
    (D) drive a long distance

18. The word "tolerance" in line 4 is closest in meaning to

    (A) endurance
    (B) fondness
    (C) phobia
    (D) superiority

19. The word "breeding" in line 13 is closest in meaning to

    (A) saving
    (B) finding
    (C) mating
    (D) keeping

20. The word "endangered" in line 16 can best be replaced by

    (A) dangerous
    (B) threatened
    (C) rare
    (D) extinct

21. As used in line 14, the phrase "at will" means

(A) by force
(B) in captivity
(C) more frequently
(D) whenever necessary

22. Where in the passage does the author mention who was responsible for bisons becoming an endangered species?

(A) Line 2
(B) Line 6
(C) Line 11
(D) Lines 15–16

23. According to the passage, all of the following are true EXCEPT

(A) some bison live on government land
(B) bisons can survive heavy snowstorms
(C) bison are primarily vegetarian
(D) the woodland bison has become extinct

QUESTIONS 24–33

Line Jupiter is the largest and most massive planet and is fifth in order of distance from the sun. It is well placed for observation for several months in every year and on average is the brightest of the planets apart from Venus, though for relatively brief periods Mars may outshine it. Jupiter's

5 less than 10-hour rotation period gives it the shortest day in the solar system insofar as the principal planets are concerned. There are no true seasons on Jupiter because the axial inclination to the perpendicular of the orbital plane is only just over 3°—less than that for any other planet.

The most famous mark on Jupiter is the Great Red Spot. It has shown

10 variations in both intensity and color, and at times it has been invisible, but it always returns after a few years. At its greatest extent it may be 40,000 kilometers long and 14,000 kilometers wide, so its surface area is greater than that of Earth. Though the latitude of the Red Spot varies little, it drifts about in longitude. Over the past century the total longitudinal drift has

15 amounted to approximately 1200°. The latitude is generally very close to -22°. It was once thought that the Red Spot might be a solid or semisolid body floating in Jupiter's outer gas. However, the Pioneer and Voyager results have refuted that idea and proven the Red Spot to be a phenomenon of Jovian meteorology. Its longevity may well be due to its

20 exceptional size, but there are signs that it is decreasing in size, and it may not be permanent. Several smaller red spots have been seen occasionally but have not lasted.

24. The main purpose of the passage is

    (A) to explain why the Great Red Spot changes
    (B) to show which of the planets shines the brightest
    (C) to give an introduction to Jupiter and its Red Spot
    (D) to prove that Jupiter is shrinking

25. According to the passage, Jupiter has the shortest day among the principal planets because

    (A) its rotation period is shorter than 10 hours
    (B) the axial inclination is only just over 3°
    (C) it is on the average the brightest of all the planets
    (D) there is the interference of the Great Red Spot

26. The author's tone in this passage is

    (A) argumentative
    (B) supportive
    (C) enthusiastic
    (D) neutral

27. According to the passage, Mars outshines Jupiter

    (A) on a regular basis
    (B) from time to time
    (C) every several months
    (D) less often than any other planet

28. This passage would be of most interest to

    (A) students of anthropology
    (B) geologists
    (C) mathematicians
    (D) amateur astronomers

29. It can be inferred from this passage that Jupiter's Great Red Spot

    (A) will become brighter with time
    (B) will one day vanish
    (C) will continue expanding
    (D) is made of floating gases

30. The word "intensity" in line 10 could best be replaced with

    (A) visibility
    (B) density
    (C) brilliance
    (D) surface area

31. According to the passage, all of the following are true about Jupiter EXCEPT

    (A) there are four planets closer to the sun
    (B) it is 14,000 kilometers wide
    (C) there is still much to be learned about the Red Spot
    (D) Pioneer and Voyager have added to our knowledge of Jupiter

32. Where in the passage does the author mention the theory about the Red Spot that has been disproved?

    (A) Lines 6-8
    (B) Lines 9-11
    (C) Lines 16-18
    (D) Lines 21-22

33. As used in line 4, the word "it" refers to

    (A) Mars
    (B) Venus
    (C) Jupiter
    (D) the sun

QUESTIONS 34-41

Line As computers have become powerful tools for the rapid and economic production of pictures, computer graphics has emerged as one of the most rapidly growing fields in computer science. It is used routinely in such diverse areas as business, industry, art, government, education, research,
5   training, and medicine.

      One of the initial uses of computer graphics, and ultimately its greatest use, has been as an aid to design, generally referred to as computer-aided design (CAD). One of its greatest advantages is that designers can see how an object will look after construction and make
10   changes freely and much more quickly than with hand drafting. For three-dimensional rendering of machine parts, engineers now rely heavily on CAD. Automobile, spacecraft, aerospace, and ship designers use CAD techniques to design vehicles and test their performance. Building designs are also created with computer graphics systems. Architects can design a
15   building layout, create a three-dimensional model, and even go for a simulated "walk" through the rooms or around the outside of the building.

      Business graphics is another rapidly growing area of computer graphics, where it is used to create graphs, charts, and cost models to
20   summarize financial, statistical, mathematical, scientific, and economic data. As an educational aid, computer graphics can be used to create weather maps and cartographic materials. Computer art also has creative and commercial art applications, where it is used in advertising, publishing, and film productions, particularly for computer animation, which is achieved by a sequential process.

34. What does the passage mainly discuss?

    (A) Routine uses of computers
    (B) Computer graphics applications
    (C) The rapidly growing field of computer science
    (D) Computers as the architects of the future

35. The word "it" in line 3 refers to

    (A) computer graphics
    (B) computer science
    (C) fields
    (D) computers

36. The paragraph following this passage would most likely be about

    (A) computer animation
    (B) flight training
    (C) cost models
    (D) applications of CAD in medicine

37. According to the passage, architects use CAD to

    (A) inspect buildings
    (B) create graphs
    (C) make cartographic materials
    (D) create three-dimensional models

38. Where in the passage does the author discuss the greatest advantage of computer-aided design?

    (A) Lines 4–8
    (B) Lines 8–10
    (C) Lines 14–17
    (D) Lines 19–22

39. According to the passage, engineers use CAD for

    (A) a simulated "walk" through model rooms
    (B) rendering machine parts
    (C) making cost models
    (D) advertising

40. The word "applications" in line 23 means

    (A) jobs
    (B) uses
    (C) creativity
    (D) layers

41. Which of the following is NOT mentioned as a use of computer graphics in business?

    (A) Charts
    (B) Cost models
    (C) Graphs
    (D) Hiring

QUESTIONS 42-50

Line   The Chumash people inhabited an area of southwestern California that
included large portions of present-day Los Angeles, Ventura, Santa Barbara,
and San Luis Obispo counties as well as the Channel Islands. They took
advantage of the rich resources of their homeland. They made great use of
5   stone for milling and for making tools and weapons. Their large domed
huts were framed by willow poles covered with mats made from twined
bulrushes harvested from the marshlands. Plant fiber was also used to
weave baskets with beautiful, intricate patterns that are regarded as being
among the finest in the world. From the trees, they used wood to make
10   bowls, bows, and several types of canoes, the largest and most durable of
which could hold up to twelve people and ply the open ocean.

    Although the Chumash were accomplished fishers and hunted a
variety of animals, including elk, antelope, deer, rabbits, and squirrels, at
least three fourths of their diet consisted of plant foods, including flowers,
15   leaves, seeds, roots, and bulbs. Their most important food source was the
acorn, from which they made flour. Plants were also used to make
medicines.

    The Chumash lived in villages that were connected by social,
political, and economic ties. A typical village consisted of several domed
20   houses, each with one or more granaries, a ceremonial dance ground, a
field for game playing, a burial ground; and one or more sweat lodges. The
Chumash were avid traders with other western tribes, who bartered for
Chumash hides, grains, fruit, beads, headdresses, nets, baskets, leather,
tools, utensils, and canoes. The Chumash even had a currency represented
25   by a string of small white shell beads. At its height the Chumash nation
consisted of 20,000 to 30,000 people, who inhabited 75 to 100 villages.

42. With which of the following topics is the author primarily concerned?

(A) A description of Chumash life
(B) The impact of the Chumash legacy
(C) An analysis of Chumash inventions
(D) Support for the Chumash nation

43. The author implies that the Chumash

(A) isolated themselves from other tribes
(B) were not artistic in nature
(C) were an industrious, inventive people
(D) were not a seafaring people

44. It can be inferred from the passage that the Chumash

(A) did not make the most of their natural resources
(B) were a highly developed people
(C) were a localized tribe
(D) lived very primitively

45. The author mentions all of the following goods the Chumash traded EXCEPT

   (A) fruit
   (B) leather
   (C) canoes
   (D) willow poles

46. According to the passage, three fourths of the Chumash diet consisted of

   (A) acorns
   (B) fish
   (C) plant foods
   (D) antelope and rabbits

47. The Chumash currency was represented by

   (A) wooden beads
   (B) tools
   (C) shells
   (D) grains

48. The passage was most probably written by a specialist in

   (A) nutrition
   (B) anthropology
   (C) ecological systems
   (D) currency and government

49. The word "intricate" in line 8 is closest in meaning to

   (A) homemade
   (B) complex
   (C) ceremonial
   (D) natural

50. The word "avid" in line 22 is closest in meaning to

   (A) hesitant
   (B) foolish
   (C) clever
   (D) eager

Directions

In this section you will read several passages. Each passage is followed by several questions. For each question choose the one best answer from (A), (B), (C), and (D). Then on your answer sheet fill in the space that corresponds to the letter you have chosen. Your answers should be based on what is stated or implied in the passage.

Read the following passage.

Some researchers distinguish primary emotions, which are thought to be universal, from secondary emotions, which include variations and blends that are specific to cultures. The primary emotions are usually identified with fear, anger, sadness, joy, surprise, and disgust. Other psychologists doubt that surprise and disgust are true emotions; they also think that this list omits universal emotions, such as love, hope, empathy, and pride, that are difficult to measure physiologically.

Example I

1. What is the main idea of the passage?
   (A) Some emotions are difficult to measure.
   (B) All emotions are universal.
   (C) A distinction is made between primary and secondary emotions.
   (D) All emotions are primary.

The main idea of the passage is that some researchers make a distinction between primary and secondary emotions. Therefore, you should choose answer (C).

Example II

1. According to the passage, other psychologists think that the emotions of surprise and disgust are

   (A) true emotions
   (B) difficult to measure
   (C) not true emotions
   (D) secondary emotions

The passage states that "other psychologists doubt that surprise and disgust are true emotions." Therefore, you should choose answer (C).

QUESTIONS 1-11

Line   Fiberscopes are one of the most important outcomes of the science of fiber optics. Fibers made of glass and transparent acrylic plastic are capable of conveying light energy, and when thousands of these fibers are combined in what is called a fiberscope, they can transmit images. The
5   most common fiberscopes contain about 750,000 fibers, each 0.001 centimeter, or 10 microns, in diameter. For certain uses, the diameter of the fiber may be as small as 5 microns.

        Fiberscopes have a wide range of applications. In the medical field, physicians use fiberscopes to examine internal organs and as an aid in
10   delicate surgeries. Miniature probes have also been developed to view muscle fiber, skin tissue, and blood cells. Fiberscopes have also found varied uses in industry, particularly to inspect or control operations in inaccessible areas. Bundles of fiberscopes fused together in a solid plate, called a faceplate, are being used in the manufacture of television picture
15   tubes and other cathode-ray tube devices.

        The most far-reaching applications of fiber-optic technology are in communications. Optical fibers carry voice messages for telephone service. The sound of the voice is electronically broken down into thousands of pulses per second, which causes a transmitting laser to send
20   coordinated pulses of light through the optical fibers. At the receiving end, the light pulses are converted to electrical signals and the voice message is reconstructed. Light-wave communication systems can handle an immensely greater number of telephone calls and television programs than the current system, and they will form the basis of the "electronic
25   superhighway" expected to crisscross the nation in the near future of the information age.

1. How do optical fibers carry voice messages?

   (A) By fusing bundles of fiberscopes into a faceplate
   (B) By converting electrical signals to light pulses
   (C) By sending coordinated electrical pulses through optical fibers
   (D) By using cathode-ray tube devices

2. Approximately how many fibers does a fiberscope contain?

   (A) 750,000
   (B) 1,000,000
   (C) 500,000
   (D) 25,000

3. The word "inaccessible" in line 13 means

   (A) difficult to find
   (B) extremely small
   (C) hard to reach
   (D) impossible to climb

4. It can be inferred from the passage that fiberscopes

   (A) have more uses in industry than in medicine
   (B) will play a major role in the information age
   (C) will decrease in importance as they become more common
   (D) have reached the peak of their development

5. Where in the passage does the author discuss the uses of miniature probes in medicine?

   (A) Lines 2-10
   (B) Lines 8-11
   (C) Lines 20-23
   (D) Lines 24-26

6. The main topic of the passage is

   (A) The birth of the "electronic superhighway"
   (B) The various applications of fiber-optic technology
   (C) How fiberscopes have enhanced the field of medicine
   (D) How sound may be transformed into light

7. As used in line 24, the word "they" refers to

   (A) fiberscopes
   (B) light-wave communication systems
   (C) television programs
   (D) telephone calls

8. The word "particularly" in line 12 is closest in meaning to

   (A) delicately
   (B) generally
   (C) visually
   (D) specifically

9. The word "coordinated" in line 20 is closest in meaning to

   (A) separated
   (B) organized
   (C) transformed
   (D) deconstructed

10. Fiberscopes are being used to do all of the following EXCEPT

    (A) assist in delicate surgeries
    (B) control operations in inaccessible areas
    (C) convert light pulses to electrical signals
    (D) transmit images

11. The passage will most likely be followed by a discussion of

    (A) homes and businesses of the future
    (B) the structure of fiberscopes
    (C) additional uses of fiberscopes in industry
    (D) the use of fiber optics in the electronic superhighway

QUESTIONS 12-23

Line   Amy Tan, the American-born daughter of Chinese immigrants, received
the Commonwealth Club Gold Award in 1989 for her first work of fiction,
the best-selling *Joy Luck Club*. The sixteen interrelated stories that
constitute the work alternate between the tales of four Chinese immigrant
5   mothers and their Americanized daughters, in an exploration of the
generational and cultural tensions experienced by many first-generation
daughters of immigrants.

   Tan's parents, like many immigrants, had high expectations for their
children and often set confusing standards, expecting Amy and her two
10   brothers to think like Chinese but to speak perfect English, excel
academically, and take advantage of every circumstance that might lead to
success. Tan, however, rebelled against her parents' expectations, which
included such exalted professions as neurosurgery, and devoted herself to
being thoroughly American and dreaming of being a fiction writer.

15   Tan obtained a bachelor's degree in English and linguistics and a
master's degree in linguistics and eventually established herself as a highly
successful business writer. Tan, however, was not satisfied despite her
material success. Turning to her life long dream, she wrote her first short
story, "Endgame," and then a second, "Waiting between the Trees." In
20   1987 Tan visited her half-sisters in China with her mother, a trip that
proved to be a turning point in her life and career. Tan felt a send of
completeness, a bonding with the country and its culture that she had
never expected. Returning from China, Tan was surprised to learn that on
the strength of her short stories she had received an advance from a
25   publisher. Tan closed her business and wrote the remaining stories for the
Joy Luck Club. It was a resounding success, well received by the critics
and appearing on the New York Times bestseller list. It has been translated
into seventeen languages, including Chinese, and was made into a movie
in 1993.

12. What is the author's main purpose in this passage?

(A) To analyze Amy Tan's literary works
(B) To support Amy Tan's decision to become a fiction writer
(C) To present biographical information about Amy Tan
(D) To criticize Amy Tan's rebellion against her parents

13. According to the passage, Amy Tan's visit to China

(A) was disappointing
(B) had a profound affect on her
(C) was not surprising in the least
(D) was a trip she had always dreamed of taking

14. In line 4, the words "the work" refer to

(A) stories
(B) writing
(C) Commonwealth Club Gold Award
(D) *Joy Luck Club*

15. Before becoming a fiction writer, Amy Tan was a successful

(A) business writer
(B) publisher
(C) English teacher
(D) neurosurgeon

16. The expectations of Tan's parents included all of the following EXCEPT

(A) excelling academically
(B) speaking perfect English
(C) questioning tradition
(D) choosing an important profession

17. It can be inferred from the passage that

(A) Tan's parents understood her dilemma but wanted the best for her
(B) it took Tan a while to summon the courage to pursue her dreams
(C) Tan started writing fiction in order to make more money
(D) Tan had always wanted to return to China

18. The word "exalted" in line 13 means

(A) highly respected
(B) very difficult
(C) common
(D) established

19. It can be concluded from this passage that

    (A) parents don't know what's best for their children
    (B) Tan did not use personal experience in her writing
    (C) Tan made the right decision when she closed her business
    (D) Tan always knew she was Chinese foremost and American only in her imagination

20. The words "rebelled against" in line 12 is closest in meaning to

    (A) defied
    (B) forgot
    (C) worked toward
    (D) failed

21. The word "resounding" in line 26 is closest in meaning to

    (A) minimal
    (B) huge
    (C) certain
    (D) potential

22. As used in line 24, the word "advance" means

    (A) offer
    (B) congratulations
    (C) message
    (D) payment

23. The word "tensions" in line 6 is closest in meaning to

    (A) confusions
    (B) conflicts
    (C) advantages
    (D) stories

QUESTIONS 24-33

Line Maine's jagged ribbon of rocky coastline was fashioned over millennia by the violent forces of the inner earth. Earthquakes and volcanic eruptions lifted and crumbled plains to form mountains that again rose and fell as molten materials welled up in huge bulges that solidified into the granitic
5   rocks typical of the Northeast. Huge glaciers also sculpted the coast, scraping and chiseling the land's features as' they passed on their way to the sea. The weight of the glaciers, estimated to have been between 1 and 2 miles thick, pressed down the entire landmass beneath. Meanwhile, melting glaciers raised the sea level by 400 feet, in essence
10   drowning the coast and forming thousands of islands, fjords, and bays.

         Beneath the sea a long, gentle underwater slope formed, on which was deposited the mud, sand, and stony debris moved seaward from the continent by the glaciers and carried by rivers. This continental shelf falls

gradually outward and downward, in some places for hundreds of miles,
15 to a depth of about 600 feet before dropping in to the ocean's depth. Ideal
conditions for abundant marine life make the riches of the continental
shelf unparalleled. Aided by the cold Labrador current, which is saturated
with oxygen and minerals, the shelf provides the perfect environment for
diatoms. Diatoms are tiny plants that form the base of the oceanic food
20 chain. In the shallow water of the shelf, these minute plants receive the
sunlight they need for photosynthesis, especially on long summer days,
when their blooms carpet the ocean floor. This immense quantity of food
supports vast shoals of shrimp, herring, and other small fish, which in turn
are food for the larger fish that are part of the legendary abundance of the
Northeast's continental shelf.

24. With which of the following topics is the author primarily concerned?

(A) The effect of the movement of ice sheets on the shape of the land
(B) The islands off the Maine coast
(C) The formation and characteristics of the Northeast coast
(D) The riches of the continental shelf

25. Which of the following is NOT mentioned as having affected the
creation of Maine's rocky coastline?

(A) Earthquakes
(B) Glaciers
(C) Ocean currents
(D) Volcanic eruptions

26. In lines 9-10, why does the author use the phrase "in essence drowning
the coast" to discuss the effects of melting glaciers?

(A) To show the devastating nature of glaciers
(B) To describe how the rising sea level covered the coastal land
(C) To support the notion that animal life was lost when the glaciers
melted
(D) To indicate the importance of natural disasters

27. What are the "ideal conditions" the author is referring to in lines 15–16?

(A) A 600-foot drop into the ocean's depth
(B) A cold current saturated with oxygen and minerals
(C) Blooms carpeting the ocean floor
(D) Diatoms existing in the shallow water of the shelf

28. The word "unparalleled" in line 17 means

(A) rivaled
(B) not original
(C) imperceptible
(D) not equaled

29. According to the passage, at what time of year are diatoms in the greatest abundance?

    (A) Spring
    (B) Summer
    (C) Autumn
    (D) Winter

30. What forms the base of the oceanic food chain?

    (A) Shrimp and herring
    (B) Oxygen and minerals
    (C) Small fish
    (D) Diatoms

31. The passage implies that the continental shelf

    (A) drops suddenly to the ocean floor
    (B) causes earthquakes and volcanic eruptions
    (C) promotes an abundance of marine life
    (D) is exposed directly to the air

32. The passage suggests that

    (A) granite indicates volcanic eruptions in the past
    (B) volcanoes scraped and chiseled the coastline
    (C) volcanoes press down on the land mass
    (D) glaciers are always accompanied by volcanoes

33. Where in the passage does the author discuss the sea level being raised?

    (A) Lines 2–3
    (B) Lines 8–9
    (C) Lines 12–13
    (D) Lines 18–19

QUESTIONS 34–41

Line   The United States Constitution established a political system comprising a national and federal government. The new federal system accommodated the thirteen original state governments while establishing new bodies and powers designed to address national concerns. The national government
5   created by the union of states stood above the state governments in specific national matters while acknowledging the role of the states or sharing power with them in other areas. State officials were required to take an oath to support the Constitution, and state courts were required to recognize the Constitution and the laws and treaties made under it as the
10 supreme law.
      The Constitution, a veritable work of genius, greatly enhanced the power of central government but carefully divided its functions into three distinct branches—executive, legislative, and judicial. The principle of

separation of powers was applied throughout the document. Carefully
15 measured checks and balances were inserted to prevent the acquisition or
concentration of power in any one branch and also for the purpose of
protecting minority rights from the potential rule of the majority. In their
powers to amend the Constitution and to elect the president and members
of the Senate, the states also gained a role in applying checks and balances.

34. In line 7, the word "them" refers to

(A) national matters
(B) the states
(C) state officials
(D) national and federal government

35. According to the passage, state officials were required to take an oath to

(A) recognize the Constitution as a work of genius
(B) share power with the federal government
(C) support the Constitution
(D) protect minority rights

36. The word "amend" in line 18 could best be replaced by

(A) change
(B) balance
(C) enhance
(D) construct

37. The author of the passage is probably an expert in

(A) social science
(B) minority issues
(C) public housing
(D) political science

38. Where in the passage does the author describe the three branches of
government?

(A) Lines 8–9
(B) Lines 15–16
(C) Line 17–18
(D) Line 19

39. The author's attitude toward the Constitution is one of

(A) humor
(B) indifference
(C) commendation
(D) disapproval

40. It can be concluded from the passage that the authors of the Constitution

   (A) intended above all to preserve the unity of the states
   (B) wanted to avoid usurpation of power by any individual or body
   (C) provided the states with the most power to govern
   (D) didn't believe that the state and federal branches of the government could work well together

41. What is the author's main purpose in the passage?

   (A) To discuss one of the principal elements of the Constitution
   (B) To mention the roles of state officials in government
   (C) To persuade the state legislators to support the Constitution
   (D) To summarize the role of the Senate

QUESTIONS 42-50

Line   Living on land, however, are the land turtles, properly called tortoises, of
       which there are approximately forty different kinds. Of these, *Gopherus,*
       including the three gopher tortoises, is found in the southern United States
       as far west as New Mexico. Gopher tortoises are so called because they dig
5   long burrows, which may be nearly 50 feet long and provide a hone for
       many other animals, such as frogs, snakes, and borrowing owls. They are
       primarily vegetarians, feeding on grass and leaves. Berlandier's tortoise, a
       slow-moving inhabitant of the arid lands of southern Texas and Mexico, is
       especially fond of prickly-pear cactus.
10   The true tortoises come to water only to drink or bathe, and they are
       adapted to walking on land by their club-shaped feet. Their limbs are
       covered with hard scales that often have a bony core. The shell is
       high-domed in all but a very few forms. The openings at the front and rear
       of the shell are usually neatly closed by the retracted limbs, on which the
15   er.arged scales may be defensively augmented with still larger spines. The
       head can be entirely withdrawn, the elbows meeting in the middle in front
       of it and the claws of the forelimbs overlapping the lower edge of the
       opening at the front. The hard-scaled soles of the hind feet cover the
       openings at the rear.
20   Tortoises have become symbols of leisurely movement, of longevity,
       and of persistence, as in Aesop's fable of the hare and the tortoise. All
       tortoises share the ability to live to a great age, but the longest life of any
       tortoise of which there is an authentic record is of a great tortoise of the
       Seychelles Islands, whose age was known to be not less than 180 years.

42. What is the main topic of the passage?

   (A) The characteristics of land turtles
   (B) The life spans of tortoises
   (C) The difference between the forty different kinds of land turtles
   (D) The symbolism associated with tortoises

43. Which of the following is NOT mentioned as a characteristic of tortoises?

(A) They have retracting limbs.
(B) They are well adapted to water.
(C) Their heads can be entirely withdrawn into the shell.
(D) They have long lives.

44. The word "their" in line 11 refers to

(A) feet
(B) limbs
(C) scales
(D) tortoises

45. Gopher tortoises primarily eat

(A) frogs
(B) snakes
(C) grass and leaves
(D) prickly-pear cactus

46. The word "augmented" in line 15 could best be replaced by

(A) added
(B) contained
(C) restricted
(D) enhanced

47. The passage preceding this one is probably about

(A) snails
(B) water turtles
(C) burrowing animals
(D) owls

48. The word "authentic" in line 23 is closest in meaning to

(A) written
(B) historic
(C) genuine
(D) legendary

49. It can be inferred from the passage that tortoises

(A) are very aggressive
(B) have a strong defense
(C) are very vulnerable
(D) may soon be extinct

50. According to the passage, how did the gopher tortoise get its name?

(A) From its diet consisting mainly of gophers
(B) From one of Aesop's fables
(C) From being a vegetarian
(D) From digging long burrows

ANSWERS

Chapter 1: Reading for Details

Introducing Details

Exercise 1
1. The passage is about hairstyles in ancient times.
2. the Middle East
3. cut in neat geometric layers
4. position, employment
5. fake beards
6. The early Greeks
7. The Romans
8. Lines 7-8
9. Line 15-16
10. Lines 21-22
11. women
12. blond
13. Greeks

Exercises on Details

Exercise 2
1. C
2. A
3. D
4. B
5. C
6. A
7. B
8. A
9. D
10. B
11. A
12. C
13. C
14. A
15. D
16. D
17. B
18. D
19. C
20. A
21. C
22. B
23. D
24. C
25. A
26. C
27. B
28. D
29. A
30. C
31. C
32. B
33. D
34. C
35. A
36. D
37. C
38. B
39. D
40. A
41. B
42. D
43. A
44. C
45. B
46. D
47. C
48. C
49. A

Exercise 3
1. B
2. B
3. A
4. C
5. C
6. B
7. B
8. B
9. C
10. A
11. A
12. C
13. B

Chapter 2: Reading for Reference and Vocabulary

Introducing Reference and Vocabulary

Exercise 1
1. The passage is about the causes, or creation, of weather.
2. Winds are caused by air moving from a high-pressure area to a low-pressure area.
3. High- and low-pressure air masses travel the globe and cause major weather changes.
4. When rising warm air meets cool air, clouds and rain are created.
5. Weather forecasters watch the movement of warm and cold air masses and try to predict how they will behave.

6. fog
7. blizzard
8. stars
9. "It" in line 4 refers to the rising air.
10. "Them" in line 7 refers to the pressure centers.
11. "Their" in line 16 refers to clouds.
12. The word "intense" in line 11 means extremely large and strong. The word severe in line 11 is similar in meaning.
13. In line 14, when air condenses, it forms water droplets. As used in the passage, condenses means to condensate, to become heavier and more compact, thus forming a liquid from vapor.
14. In lines 15-16, when clouds reach a saturation point, or the point at which they can no longer contain their moisture, the droplets fall to Earth as rain or snow.
15. Sophisticated instruments are advanced, often complicated machines. Some examples of sophisticated instruments we now use in everyday life are computers, watches with digital readouts, VCRs, and cellular phones.

Exercises on Reference and Vocabulary
Exercise 2
1. D
2. A
3. C
4. B
5. B
6. B
7. D
8. A
9. C
10. D
11. B
12. C
13. B
14. C

Exercise 3
1. D
2. B
3. D
4. A
5. C
6. B
7. C
8. B
9. A
10. B
11. B
12. D
13. D

14. C
15. C
16. B
17. B
18. D
19. B
20. C
21. D
22. B
23. C
24. C
25. B
26. D
27. C
28. D
29. B
30. D

Chapter 3: Reading for Main Ideas
Introducing Main Ideas
Exercise 1
1. The main idea of the passage is how to lead a healthy life.
2. fat, sugar, salt
3. tiredness, irritability, poor general health
4. (any two) running, bicycle riding, swimming
5. carbohydrates
6. vitamins
7. dieting
8. walking
9. "Their" in line 17 refers to people.
10. "Nutrition" in line 4 means the food we eat.
11. The best substitute for the word "limit" in line 9 is restrict.
12. "Constantly" in line 17 means continually, or always.

Exercises on Main Ideas
Exercise 2
1. B
2. A
3. C
4. D
5. D
6. C
7. B
8. D
9. A
10. C

Chapter 4: Reading for Inference

Introducing Inference

Exercise 1

1. The passage is mainly about how the contributions of filmmakers and inventors from all over the world led to the development of motion pictures.
2. zoetrope
3. human movements
4. camera
5. celluloid film
6. Lumiere
7. movement of objects
8. patented (Thomas Edison)
9. "It" in line 6 refers to the zoetrope.
10. "They" in line 7 refers to the rotating pictures.
11. In line 7, the word merged means combined, or came together.
12. The word contributions in line 27 means offerings.
13. We can infer that Le Prince was a talented inventor who would have made a significant contribution to filmmaking had he lived longer.
14. We can infer that the motion picture camera was a complicated machine that required the invention, experimentation, and creativity of many people to develop.

Exercises on Inference

Exercise 2

1. Cannot be inferred
2. Cannot be inferred
3. Can be inferred
4. Can be inferred
5. Cannot be inferred
6. Can be inferred
7. Can be inferred
8. Can be inferred
9. Can be inferred
10. Cannot be inferred
11. Can be inferred
12. Cannot be inferred
13. Cannot be inferred
14. Cannot be inferred
15. Can be inferred
16. Cannot be inferred
17. Can be inferred
18. Cannot be inferred
19. Cannot be inferred
20. Can be inferred

Exercise 3

1. D
2. C
3. C
4. B
5. A
6. D
7. A
8. B
9. A
10. B
11. B
12. A
13. D
14. C
15. B
16. A
17. D
18. B
19. B
20. C
21. D
22. A
23. C
24. D
25. A
26. C
27. B
28. C

Chapter 5: Additional Reading Skills

Introducing Additional Reading Skills

Exercise 1

1. The passage is mainly about the reasons why skiing is a popular sport.
2. Being able to descend a hill, to turn at will, and enjoy nature at its loveliest are thrills for all age groups.
3. Snow conditions change as the temperature and weather conditions change throughout the day.
4. Skiers today wear warm, light, down-filled clothes.
5. Modern materials have made today's skis lighter, more flexible, and suited to people of all ages and abilities.
6. Snow-making equipment is used in areas with little snowfall.
7. places to ski
8. modern materials
9. In line 2, the word "thaw" means the melting of snow in spring.
10. In line 10, the word "trail" refers to the areas, or runs, that people ski.

11. Ski areas are more available today thanks to snow-making equipment in warmer climates. Mountains that once could not accommodate skiers now provide excellent ski slopes and conditions.

12. This passage would most likely be found in a ski or sport magazine.

13. (A)   favorable

14. (D)   ski resorts around the world

15. (C)   To inform

16. More people enjoy skiing today than ever before. Skiing today is easier and in some ways more enjoyable than in the past. Skiing will continue to gain in popularity.

17. (C)   The author explains the popularity of skiing and gives reasons.

Exercises on Additional Reading Skills
Exercise 2
1. B
2. D
3. C
4. C
5. D
6. A
7. C
8. D
9. A
10. C
11. C
12. B
13. A
14. C
15. A
16. A
17. D
18. C
19. C
20. D
21. B
22. C
23. B
24. A
25. C
26. B
27. A
28. A
29. D
30. B
31. A
32. A
33. B
34. D
35. D
36. B
37. B
38. D
39. C

40. A
41. D
42. C
43. C
44. D
45. B
46. D
47. C
48. B
49. D
50. D

Practice Test 1
The correct answer is indicated with an asterisk (*).

1. (A)   Although the passage does discuss the extremely high temperature of a supernova, that is only one fact about supernovas. The passage is mainly about how supernovas are formed and how powerful they are.

   *(B)   The many facts given in the passage mainly explain how supernovas are formed and how powerful they are.

   (C)   Shock waves are only one cause of supernovas. Shock waves are not the main subject of the passage.

   (D)   The density of a neutron star is one fact about a supernova, but it is not what the passage is mainly about.

2. *(A)   "It" refers to the shock wave that is moving outward. The shock wave meets the star's collapsing outer layers, which causes a catastrophic explosion.

   (B)   "It" is the shock wave within the neutron star that meets the collapsing out layers and causes a catastrophic explosion.

   (C)   The catastrophic explosion occurs when the shock wave moves outward and meets the material falling inward.

   (D)   "It" refers to the shock wave that meets the star's collapsing layers and causes a catastrophic explosion.

3. **(A)** The passage states that the 1987 supernova was "in the Large Cloud of Magellan." This statement is true.

   (B) The passage states that the 1987 supernova was 170,000 light-years away. This statement is also true.

   *(C) The passage states that the 1987 supernova "shone as a star between magnitudes 2 and 3," NOT 3 and 4. Statement C is NOT true.

   (D) The passage does state that the 1987 supernova "had a low peak luminosity by supernova standards."

   (A) Assumed means supposed to be true. It is not similar in meaning to detectable, which means able to be seen or determined as being present.

   (B) Known refers to information about something in one's mind. However, things are detectable with the senses, such as taste, hearing, sight, and smell.

   *(C) Perceptible means becoming aware of something through the senses. This word is closest in meaning to detectable, which also refers to the senses.

   (D) Audible means having used only one of the senses, hearing. This word is related to but not closest in meaning to detectable.

5. **(A)** A characteristic is a quality, trait, or feature of something. It cannot take the place of remnant, which means a remaining part of something.

   (B) A relic is something old that reminds us of the past. It is not similar in meaning to remnant.

   (C) A specter is a ghost or the spirit of something that once existed. It is not the same as remnant, which is a small part of something that was once whole.

   *(D) Both remnant and remainder mean a small remaining part or trace of something. Either word can be used without changing the meaning of the sentence.

6. **(A)** A botanist studies plants and therefore would not be the most likely author of this passage.

   (B) An economist is an expert in economics, the management of money, or other material resources. An economist would probably not be an expert on supernovas.

   (C) A mathematician deals with numbers and would not be the likely author of this passage.

   *(D) An astronomer studies the stars, planets, and other heavenly bodies. Therefore, an astronomer would be the most likely person to write about a supernova, which is "due to the collapse of a massive star."

7. **(A)** Magnitude refers to the brightness of a star. It is not similar in meaning to multitudes, which refers to a great number or quantity.

   (B) Groups refers to associations, but do not indicate a large number. Therefore, (B) is incorrect.

   *(C) Many is closest in meaning to multitudes.

   (D) Temperatures refer to a measurement of heat; the passage is not concerned with the temperature of the neutrons.

8. ***(A)** Violent is a term used to describe something that is sudden and occurs with great force. This word is closest in meaning to catastrophic.

   (B) Colorful refers to something that contains or gives off many colors. This is not an aspect of supernovas that is mentioned in the passage and is not similar in meaning to catastrophic.

   (C) The study of supernovas is a scientific type of study, but does not express the sudden and forceful nature of a star exploding.

   (D) Luminous means bright, and although brightness is certainly a factor of a supernova, it is not close in meaning to catastrophic.

9. (A) The passage states that a supernova remnant may be detectable as a pulsar. Supernovas do not happen to pulsars; pulsars are something that may be detected after a supernova has occurred.

(B) The sun is obviously still shining, and therefore has not collapsed, nor has it used up its fuel.

(C) The passage does not mention anything about stars colliding.

*(D) The first paragraph of the passage ends with a reference to a black hole. In extreme cases, a supernova remnant may be a neutron star or a black hole.

10. (A) The passage does mention that a Type II supernova occurs when a massive star collapses, but does not say that the size is the cause of the explosion. Therefore, (A) is not correct.

(B) The birth of stars is not discussed in the passage.

(C) A neutron star is formed when a star collapses. This is a stage of the supernova, but not the beginning.

*(D) When its main nuclear fuel has been used up, a massive star collapses. This is how supernovas begin.

11. (A) In line 5, the process of a supernova is about to begin.

(B) Line 8 describes the most active part of a supernova, what is left has not occurred at this point.

*(C) Line 12 states that after most of a star's material is blown away, an incredibly dense neutron star or black hole remains.

(D) Line 20 discusses the brightness of a particular supernova, not what is left of a star.

12. (A) The passage states that Pippin, a primitive artist, had a "feel for two-dimensional design." Therefore, this statement is true.

(B) The passage states that Pippin's feel for "the arrangement of colors and patterns made him one of the finest primitive artists." Statement (B) is true.

(C) It is indicated in the passage that "Pippin was not trained." Statement (C) is also true.

*(D) The passage does not mention portraits as a form of primitive art. Statement (D) is the only statement that is NOT true.

13. (A) The passage indicates that Pippin started painting and drawing after he was wounded in the war, not during World War I.

(B) The passage states that Pippin was not trained. Therefore, (B) is not correct.

(C) The passage indicates that Pippin had artistic sensitivity, but it does not mention anything about someone discussing this with Pippin.

*(D) The passage states that Pippin "discovered . . . that by keeping his right wrist steady with his left hand, he could paint and draw."

14. (A) Pippin's hometown is not mentioned in line 6.

*(B) Pippin's hometown of West Chester, Pennsylvania, is mentioned in line 10.

(C) Line 4 does not mention the name of Pippin's hometown.

(D) Line 9 discusses the scenes of people and places that Pippin painted, but it does not give the name of Pippin's hometown.

15. *(A) The passage states that Pippin painted "scenes of the people and places of his hometown of West Chester, Pennsylvania," and that his Domino Players is a scene of "four women gathered around a wooden table in a simple kitchen setting." From this it can be assumed that Pippin's life in rural West Chester was also simple and basic.

(B) The second paragraph discusses the fact that Pippin did a series of paintings on the abolitionist John Brown, but it also states that "he shied away from social issues for the most part." Pippin may have been interested in the subject of abolition, but there is nothing to indicate he was obsessed with it.

(C) Although the article states that Pippin was wounded during World War I, it does not discuss how he felt about his experiences.

(D) Because Pippin "achieved his greatest success with scenes of the people and places of his hometown," it can be inferred that Pippin liked to think about and draw scenes from his past.

16. **(A)** The purpose is the reason why something takes place. It cannot take the place of arrangement, which means the placement or order of something.

(B) A fixture is something that stays in one place and never changes. It does not mean the same as arrangement, which involves the placement of things.

*(C) Arrangement is the placement or order of something. Therefore, composition can be used in place of arrangement without changing the meaning of the sentence.

(D) A blend of things is a mixture or combination of them. It does not mean the same as arrangement.

17. **(A)** The author does state that Pippin was not trained; however, the author also declares that Pippin was "one of the finest primitive artists America has produced." Therefore, it is not likely that the author would agree with statement (A).

(B) Since the author writes about Pippin's great success as a primitive artist, it can be inferred that the author would not agree with the statement that primitive art is an excuse for lack of training and talent.

*(C) The passage states that Pippin was "one of the finest primitive artists America has produced." Therefore, the author would most likely agree with the statement that Pippin made a significant contribution to American art.

(D) The passage states that Pippin "shied away from social issues." Therefore, the author would not agree with statement (D).

18. **(A)** Anthropology is the study of cultures. Art is part of culture, and it is possible that this might be part of a required reading in anthropology. However, it is not the best answer because it is much more likely that this passage would be required reading in an art course.

(B) A drama course would most likely require the reading of plays.

(C) A sociology course may include some study of artists and how they relate to the society in which they live. However, this is not the best answer, because the passage is much more likely to be part of required reading in an art course.

*(D) This passage on an artist who lived long ago would most likely be required reading in an art history course.

19. **(A)** Educated refers to training, as in an art school, and line 4 has already stated that Pippin was not trained.

(B) Artistic can mean naturally skilled, but it most directly refers to a refined process, and is not the same as intuitive.

(C) Intense is similar to passionate, or dramatic, but is not similar in meaning to intuitive.

*(D) Instinctive describes something that comes without guidance, something done by reflex. This is the same as intuitive, which describes something inborn.

20. **(A)** To postpone something means to set it aside to be used later. Pippin did not intend to use social issues later in his paintings, so (A) is incorrect.

*(B) Avoided is closest in meaning to shied away from. Both describe not wanting anything to do with an issue. Pippin had no desire to portray social issues in his paintings.

(C) Shied away from is not a term specific to the field of painting.

(D) Fear is a strong emotional reaction to something; Pippin simply chose not to deal with social issues in his paintings. He was not afraid of them.

21. *(A)   Seated is the same as gathered, as it is used in line 11 of the passage. It is implied in the passage that the four women are sitting around the table, talking, or perhaps readying for a meal.

    (B)   Scattered means positioned randomly in relation to an object or place, some close, some far away. The women in Pippin's painting Domino Players are gathered together at the table. Therefore, (B) is not correct.

    (C)   Collected is more often used to describe something done to objects and would not be used to describe a group of people.

    (D)   Domesticated refers to someone or something grown used to spending most of its time in the home.

22. (A)   Primitive is the name of the art movement that Pippin was a part of. This is unrelated to the meaning of rural.

    (B)   Urban refers to a quality of city life, which is the opposite of rural.

    *(C)   Country means the same as rural, describing a lifestyle particular to those living away from cities, such as farmers.

    (D)   Beautiful means something pleasant to behold, and is not similar in meaning to rural.

23. (A)   Violence was not a major theme in Pippin's paintings, because the passage states that he shied away from social issues.

    (B)   A rural domestic scene would be a mother doing laundry or feeding chickens. Getting wounded in World War I cannot be described as a rural domestic scene.

    *(C)   The author includes the fact that Pippin was wounded to show that he succeeded in spite of a handicap. It is hard to succeed as an artist even without being wounded.

    (D)   Lines 4–6 state that Pippins sensitivity and skill at visual arrangement were the things that classified him as a primitive artist.

24. (A)   The passage only provides one statement about Navajo folklore; therefore, that is not what the passage is mostly about.

    (B)   Weather is discussed in the passage, but only as it relates to the spadefoot toad. Most of the information in the passage is about the toad.

    *(C)   The passage discusses the living and mating habits of the spadefoot toad. That is what the article is mainly about.

    (D)   The mating rituals of the male spadefoot are only a small part of the discussion of the life of the spadefoot toad.

25. *(A)   The passage states that the spadefoot toad "remains dormant beneath the Sonoran Desert of Arizona . . . for as long as eight or nine months."

    (B)   The first paragraph says that "with the onset of summer thunderstorms" the toads emerge "to begin their brief and frantic mating season."

    (C)   At the end of the second paragraph, the author states that the toads gorge themselves on insects. The author does not say anything about the frogs eating leaves and grasses.

    (D)   Line 13 states that the young "mature with remarkable speed." This means they develop very quickly.

26. (A)   The passage states that the spadefoot toad lies dormant for as long as eight or nine months. That means it is active only three to four months a year. Statement (A) is true.

    (B)   The passage states that the female spadefoot lays "as many as 1,000 eggs in a small pool of life-sustaining rainwater."

    *(C)   The second paragraph mentions that spadefoot toads are also threatened by "devouring insects and animals." Therefore, the desert sun in not the spadefoot's only enemy. Statement (C) is NOT true.

    (D)   The author writes that "those lucky enough to survive develop through each tadpole stage." It can be inferred from this that many tadpoles die before they reach maturity.

27. (A) Although the spadefoot remains dormant during the desert's eight or nine dry months, the passage gives no further information regarding how long the spadefoot could survive without rain.

(B) The Navajo legend about toads falling from the sky was based upon what appeared to occur rather than on what the Navajo actually observed.

*(C) The spadefoot has certain habits that allow it to survive the heat and drought of the Sonoran Desert. Therefore, it can be concluded that spadefoot toads are well adapted to their environment.

(D) The statement "those lucky enough to survive develop through each tadpole stage" leads the reader to conclude that the chances of a tadpole's becoming an adult are not very great.

28. (A) A botanist studies plants and would therefore not likely be the author of this passage.

*(B) Since a biologist studies plant and animal life, a biologist would probably be the author of this article.

(C) A chemist is trained in the study of the composition and chemical properties of substances. A chemist would not be the likely author of this passage.

(D) Since a geographer is an expert on the earth's physical features, it is not likely that a geographer would be writing about frogs.

29. (A) Since the weather of the Sonoran Desert is only a small part of this article on the spadefoot toad, it is unlikely that the passage following this would be about weather.

(B) The article is about how the spadefoot adapts to its environment. Reproduction is only one aspect of the story. It is not likely that the reproductive habits of insects would follow this article.

(C) Since there is no mention of the dwellings of the Navajo people, it is unlikely the passage would be followed by a discussion of Navajo dwellings.

*(D) Since the main subject of the article is how the spadefoot toad adapts to its desert environment, the article is very likely to be followed by a discussion on other desert animals and their abilities to adapt to their environment.

30. (A) Line 7 states that the mating season is brief, therefore lengthy is incorrect.

*(B) Excited is the same as frantic, indicating a sense of urgency and much activity done in very little time.

(C) Froglike means resembling a frog, and is not close in meaning to frantic.

(D) Things done in a frantic way can involve danger, but danger is not implied simply by describing something as frantic.

31. (A) Weather is only one of the elements, or conditions, affecting the survival of the toad.

(B) Time cannot be used in place of elements, which means the natural conditions, or environment, in which the young toads hatch and mature.

*(C) Elements, as used in this passage, refers to the physical conditions, or environment, in which the toads fight for survival.

(D) The elements mentioned in the passage are heat and devouring insects and animals. Thunderstorms are not mentioned as one of the elements affecting the survival of the spadefoot toad.

32. (A) Mating refers to reproducing and is not similar to gorging.
    (B) The spadefoot toads dig a hole to live in during the drought, but no gorging occurs at this time
    (C) The toads gorge on insects to build up energy for their time underground. This is not the same as enjoying.
    *(D) Devouring something means to consume it, or use it as food. This is the word most similar to gorging.

33. (A) Line 1 mentions the Navajo people, but nothing about location is stated.
    (B) Line 9 describes the spadefoot sitting in a muddy pool; this does not state where they are geographically.
    *(C) Lines 3-4 refer to the Sonoran Desert of Arizona, which is the geographic location of the spadefoot toads.
    (D) Lines 16-17 mention no locations.

34. *(A) Lines 4-7 define joint-stock companies as companies "in which each member was responsible for the obligations of the mutual enterprise."
    (B) There is no mention of joint-stock companies in lines 10-12.
    (C) Lines 13-16 do not discuss joint-stock companies.
    (D) There is no mention of joint-stock companies in lines 20-24.

35. (A) The second paragraph states that "America's first private commercial bank . . . was chartered by Congress on December 31, 1781."
    (B) The passage states that the early banks were "local and limited."
    *(C) The first paragraph mentions that the origin of banking "was not an over-night phenomenon." Therefore, it is NOT true that banking developed rapidly in the United States.
    (D) Lines 18-19 state that "the first national bank . . . opened its main office in Philadelphia."

36. (A) The first paragraph says that "commercial corporations didn't make their appearance until the early to mid-1700s." Therefore, they appeared before, not after, 1800.
    (B) If commercial corporations made their appearance in the early to mid-1700s, they were not in existence before the 1600s.
    *(C) Because the passage says that commercial corporations appeared in the early to mid-1700s, they would have appeared sometime around 1750.
    (D) The year 1791 is the late 1700s. The passage states that commercial corporations made their appearance in the early to mid-1700s.

37. (A) The third paragraph discusses the merger of railroads, utilities, and factories, but it was the investment banking houses that promoted these mergers and also "provided the capital for expansion."
    (B) The establishment of the Federal Reserve System is only one fact presented in the article. It is not what the article is mostly about.
    (C) The article does discuss how early joint-stock companies were "principally nonprofit corporations," but this is also not the main topic of the passage.
    *(D) All three paragraphs in this passage present facts about how banks and corporations developed in the United States. That is what the passage is mainly about.

38. *(A) "All these banks" refers to the three private commercial banks mentioned in lines 15-17, the Bank of North America, the Bank of New York, and the Bank of Massachusetts.
(B) National banking is mentioned in line 18. "All these banks" refers to the private commercial banks mentioned in lines 15-17.
(C) Investment banking houses are mentioned in the third paragraph. "All these banks" refers to the private commercial banks discussed in the second paragraph.
(D) Nonprofit corporations are mentioned in the first paragraph. "All these banks" refers to the private commercial banks discussed in the second paragraph.

39. (A) Lines 7-8 continue discussing the subject of corporations.
*(B) Line 15 marks the point at which the author moves from the subject of corporations to the subject of banks.
(C) Line 20 provides additional information about banks. It does not mark the point at which the author's focus changes from corporations to banks.
(D) Line 25 discusses the establishment of the Federal Reserve System.

40. (A) Phenomenon in this passage refers to the origin, or beginning, of banking and capital markets. Factor would not be a good substitute for phenomenon.
*(B) An occurrence is something that happens or takes place. It could replace phenomenon, which refers to the appearance of banking and capital markets that took place in the United States.
(C) Development has to do with changes that occur over time. It would not be a good substitute for phenomenon, which refers to the birth, or appearance, of banking and capital markets.
(D) An examination is a very close look at or inspection of something. It could not replace phenomenon in this passage.

41. (A) Building materials are not similar in meaning to capital. Building materials are bought with capital.
(B) A word that sounds the same as capital, capitol, refers to a large city. This is the wrong kind of capital.
*(C) Capital and financial resources mean the same thing. Other terms that are similar in meaning are assets and funds.
(D) The corporate structure is not the same as capital. Capital is very important to the corporate structure, however.

42. (A) The passage mentions the contribution the telegraph made to journalism, but it does not discuss the history of journalism.
(B) Details about the origin of the national telegraph network are provided in the passage, but that is not what the passage is mostly about.
(C) The fact that the telegraph contributed to the expansion of railroads is discussed in the article. However, that is also not what the article is mainly about.
*(D) The passage is mainly concerned with the development of the national telegraph network and the contributions it made to the communications industry.

43. (A) The passage states that San Francisco was added to the network, but does not discuss how this enhanced the business of news gathering.
*(B) Lines 14-15 mentions that the telegraph allowed for more timely reporting and expanded the amount of information a newspaper could supply.
(C) The expansion of the railroads is discussed earlier in the passage. How this is related to news gathering is not explored.
(D) The telegraph provided an efficient means to monitor schedules and routes for the railroads, but the effect of this on the business of news gathering is not stated.

44. (A) The author mentions that the combination of the extension of the telegraph and the invention of the rotary printing press revolutionized the world of journalism. The author's purpose is to show how the communications industry was affected by these inventions. The author does not compare the inventions.

(B) The author gives details about the origins of the communications industry. The passage is concerned with the past, not the present or future.

ʼ(C) The author uses details to support the main topic, which is how the electric telegraph gave birth to and revolutionized the communications industry.

(D) The author states that "Samuel B. Morse succeeded in making the invention useful." The author is praising, not criticizing, Morse.

45. (A) There are no company names mentioned in the passage. Therefore, (A) is not correct.

(B) The West Coast refers to the western part of the United States, such as California.

ʼ(C) The Rockies is a mountain range that extends from the North into New Mexico. The author uses the mountains to show that the telegraph reached not only across large distances, but other types of obstacles.

(D) There are no railroad companies mentioned.

46. (A) Because the electric telegraph "gave birth to the communications industry," its inventor, Samuel B. Morse, made a significant contribution.

ʼ(B) The passage states that although Samuel B. Morse succeeded in making the telegraph useful in 1837, it was not until six years later, in 1843, that "the first telegraph line of consequence was constructed." It can be inferred from this that it took some time before the telegraph achieved its full potential.

(C) Had the telegraph not been invented, it could never have been extended. Therefore, it cannot be inferred that one is more important than the other.

(D) The passage states that "the invention of the electric telegraph gave birth to the communications industry."

47. (A) Although revolution indicates the presence of considerable change to something, it is usually associated with positive change. Destroyed is not appropriate.

(B) Revolution can mean to revolve around something, but as used in the passage, it refers to sweeping changes.

(C) Gathered means brought together, which is not close in meaning to revolutionized.

ʼ(D) Transformed means changed from a former state in an extreme way, and is similar in meaning to revolutionized. (D) is correct.

48. (A) The passage states that Morse invented the telegraph in 1837. (A) is true.

(B) Lines 5-6 states that in the year after 1860, people could use the telegraph in San Francisco. This statement is true.

ʼ(C) Lines 9-12 states that the telegraph combined with the printing press revolutionized the world of journalism. It does not state that the telegraph lead to the printing press.

(D) The passage discusses how the telegraph fortified the ties between East and West.

49. **(A)** In line 13, gathering refers to the preceding word, news. It refers to information, not people.
    •(B) Journalism is the business of news gathering. Gathering refers to news or information.
    (C) Journalists are in the business of gathering news, or information. In this passage, gathering does not refer to objects.
    (D) In line 13, gathering refers to the preceding word, news, which refers to information. It does not refer to any substances.

50. **•(A)** The passage provides historical facts about the effects of the electric telegraph on communication and transportation in nineteenth-century America. The passage would most likely appear in a book on U.S. history.
    (B) Although the article does mention how the electric telegraph contributed to the rapid expansion of the railroads, it is only one detail in a passage concerned with the historical contributions of the electric telegraph. That detail might appear in a book on trains, but it is not likely that the entire passage would be found there.
    (C) A science textbook would be more likely to discuss how Samuel Morse invented the telegraph than how the telegraph contributed to the birth of the communications industry.
    (D) It is not very likely that a computer magazine would contain a passage on the development of the telegraph.

Practice Test 2

1. C
2. D
3. A
4. C
5. A
6. B
7. D
8. A
9. C
10. A
11. A
12. D
13. B
14. D
15. B
16. B
17. A
18. B
19. C
20. D
21. A
22. C
23. B
24. A
25. D
26. B
27. C
28. A
29. C
30. B
31. A
32. C
33. D
34. B
35. A
36. B
37. D
38. C
39. B
40. D
41. B
42. B
43. B
44. D
45. A
46. B
47. D
48. D
49. B
50. C

Practice Test 3

1. B
2. C
3. C
4. D
5. C
6. D
7. A
8. C
9. C
10. C
11. D
12. C
13. C
14. D
15. B
16. C
17. D
18. D
19. B
20. B
21. A
22. C
23. D
24. B
25. A
26. D
27. C
28. B
29. A
30. C
31. B
32. A
33. C
34. C
35. A
36. D
37. D
38. A
39. B
40. A
41. C
42. D
43. C
44. A
45. C
46. B
47. D
48. A
49. C
50. D

Practice Test 4

1. D
2. A
3. C
4. A
5. B
6. C
7. D
8. C
9. C
10. B
11. A
12. D
13. D
14. C
15. A
16. B
17. B
18. A
19. C
20. B
21. D
22. C
23. D
24. C
25. A
26. D
27. B
28. D
29. B
30. A
31. B
32. C
33. C
34. B
35. A
36. A
37. D
38. B
39. B
40. B
41. D
42. A
43. C
44. B
45. D
46. C
47. C
48. B
49. B
50. D

Practice Test 5

1.	B
2.	A
3.	C
4.	B
5.	B
6.	B
7.	B
8.	D
9.	B
10.	C
11.	D
12.	C
13.	B
14.	D
15.	A
16.	C
17.	B
18.	A
19.	C
20.	A
21.	B
22.	D
23.	B
24.	C
25.	C

26.	B
27.	B
28.	D
29.	B
30.	D
31.	C
32.	A
33.	B
34.	B
35.	C
36.	A
37.	D
38.	C
39.	C
40.	B
41.	A
42.	A
43.	B
44.	D
45.	C
46.	D
47.	B
48.	C
49.	B
50.	D

NOTES